JOSEPHINE

SINGER, DANCER, SOLDIER, SPY

EILIDH MCGINNESS

JOSEPHINE

Singer, dancer, soldier, SPY.

By

Eilidh McGinness

First published in 2019
By Eilidh McGinness
ISBN
1916245307
A catalogue record of this book is available from the British Library.

AUTHOR'S NOTE

This book aims to use the techniques of a novel to tell the story of the work Josephine Baker carried out for the French Resistance during WW2.

The characters in the pages which follow are not wholly fictional and much of what occurs in the novel occurred in some form in real life.

In order to transform historical events into a novel it has been necessary to simplify some matters and dramatize and invent other matters.

I hope you enjoy reading about Josephine and her companions adventures during this terrible period in history.
There are additional pictures and maps available at Pinterest
https://www.pinterest.fr/eilidhmcginness1/

Eilidh McGinness

2019

PROLOGUE

At first there is only darkness. Then tiny buttons of light. Finally becoming flaming torches. One followed by another. Gripped in hands held high by figures cloaked in white. An eerie silence hangs over the scene. It is part of it. Part of the drama which is about to unfold. There are no words. They are not needed. Those who wait, know what is to come, without knowing, without words, without consciousness.

A dawn light creeps across the sky, revealing from the shadows a gathered crowd, thousands of men, women and children, waiting expectantly, in silence, for the promised spectacle.

A wooden platform rises several feet above the audience's heads, like a remote desert island on a becalmed sea. Centrally positioned on the construction, a pole perhaps six feet in height. The torch-bearers move slowly towards the platform with the solemnity of a regal procession. The crowd divides, clearing a passageway before them in a silent expectant ripple.

Screams shatter the silence.

Then a woman's screeching. "He don't know what he gone and said. He ain't got the means. He my son. I know he ain't done what he said. He don't know how."

A woman wearing a simple dress tugs at the white robe of the figure leading the procession. The flickering torchlight illuminates her black face, wet with tears. The terror in her eyes shines as vividly as the flames. The screams are hers. Her pleas fall like rain on the gathered crowd, but they do not listen. She is the only player in the drama not wearing a mask.

A man in the crowd steps forward, and there is an ominous thud as his baton cracks against her skull. She drops to the ground.

Silence.

The robed figures form into a circle surrounding the platform, framing it, as if it were a picture, as the early morning light begins to dispel the darkness.

The leader passes his torch to a tall man, smartly dressed, as if for church, who is closest to the platform. Then he climbs up the wooden steps, lifting his robes as he does so, revealing brown leather shoes of good quality. He is followed by several other cloaked figures who stand with their torches

held above their heads. The leader raises his hands and walks around the stage. The crowd remains silent. Expectant. The figure beckons with his hand, reaching out as though an ancient druid summoning a sacred spirit. Suddenly, there is a burst of activity. A man is dragged forward to the foot of the platform and then onto the stage. He is black. He struggles violently against the bonds securing his wrists behind his back, to no avail.

The gag over his mouth slips free and he shouts, "Help me! Help me!"

His voice is urgent. Desperate.

Silence answers him. The crowd watches, unmoved by his pleas.

Two hooded figures move forward and place a noose around the man's neck. They jerk him back against the pole and tie him to it.

The man's struggles intensify. There is a choking sound.

Voices erupt from the silent spectators. Demands for punishment,, retribution, warning. This would be no easy death.

The figure, slowly twisting the rope tighter around the man's neck, stops. Awaiting instruction. The leader steps forward, his grand master's necklet gleams as the gold reflects the dawn rays. He grabs hold of the prisoner's shirt and rips it from his body. The crowd cheers. He holds a cleaver high above his head.

Its steel glints in the flames.

The crowd yells encouragement. The grand master

signals to the other robed figures on the platform. As if one body, they move and grip the prisoner's hand. The man screams. The grand master holds up the prisoner's right thumb. He has amputated it. The crowd cheers and waves. The leader passes the bloodied digit to a teenager who has climbed up the steps seeking a souvenir.

The procedure is repeated again and again. Only after the most brutal amputation do the crowd seem sated.

A preacher appears on the platform. His words are drowned by the taunts from the crowd. Kerosene is poured over the prisoner and he is left alone on the stage. A torch is tossed onto the platform.

The prisoner is heard to sing, "O Lord I'm a coming" as the flames lick around him. The platform collapses.

Silence.

It is over. The crowd disperses as silently as it formed. A poster advertising the lynching of Moses Smith flutters in the wind before being consumed by the fire.

It is the third of June 1906, St Louis, Missouri, USA. Close by Freda Josephine McDonald is born into poverty, into a world where white men rule. Within twenty years, she will be one of the richest women in the world.

PART I

SINGER

DANCER

Image Josephine Baker

JOSEPHINE BAKER
GLOBE PHOTOS, INC.

Chapter 1

THE HOSPITAL, ST LOUIS, MISSOURI, 1913

"What you gone and done now, girl?" Carrie McDonald boomed as her robust figure appeared at the ward entrance. Josephine shrunk down under the covers. Her mother always seemed blissfully unaware of just how black she was. White faces, mouths open, followed her mother's progress as she approached Josephine's bed as surely as a homing pigeon within sight of its destination. Even the nurses stopped and stared.

"What you gone and done?" she asked again. Josephine rolled her eyes and grinned in an effort to hide her humiliation.

"Excuse me, Mrs McDonald," interrupted the ward nurse in a tone that brooked no argument. "Doctor Marshall needs to see you immediately. Follow me, please?"

Carrie McDonald glared at Josephine before following the nurse, muttering under her breath as she went. She was shown to a chair in one of the hospital corridors and told to wait.

"I want to see my daughter."

"After the doctor has spoken to you," the nurse responded curtly as she walked off.

Carrie sat peaceably enough for the first half hour. Then she began to stalk up and down the corridor. And then she made her way back to the ward where she had found Josephine.

"Come on, girl, it's time to go home", she shouted from the ward entrance.

"Please, Mrs McDonald, the doctor needs to speak to you." The nurse blocked the path to Josephine's bed.

"I can't sit in no corridor all day. And that girl's got work to go to. I just come to take her home. I don't need to be taking up no doctor's time."

"Really, Mrs McDonald, it is very important."

A tall, grey-haired and bespectacled man, wearing a white coat appeared. The nurse sighed with relief. "Here he is now." The doctor approached them, having noticed Carrie immediately. For how could he not?

"Mrs McDonald. You are Josephine's mother?"

"Of course I am."

"A word please." He nodded towards the child. "In private. Will you follow me?"

They walked out of the ward and into the corridor. The doctor turned around.

"Mrs MacDonald, I have examined your daughter. I understand that she stood on a nail or some such item while walking barefoot. Unfortunately, her foot has become infected. I'm afraid we will have to amputate her foot from just above the ankle. I can carry out the operation later today and you will be able to collect her tomorrow."

Carrie McDonald paled, silenced momentarily as she absorbed the implications of the doctor's words.

"I don't understand," she blustered. "There must be a mistake. Something that can be done. Please, doctor."

"No mistake. The operation is urgent. She doesn't live with you. Is that correct?"

"Yes, she works for Mrs Wilson. She lives with her. Has done for some time."

"And can she return there to recuperate?"

"Only if she is working. She ain't gonna work with no foot, is she? She ain't gonna dance on one leg."

"If you can guarantee that she will be in a clean, healthy environment, I could try to avoid the amputation, but it would put her life at risk. Can you guarantee that her foot

would be bathed in sterile water every day? Clean bandages?

Disinfected surroundings? You do have a room for her at your home, I presume."

"We ain't got nothing, doctor. We got one room for the whole family. We got tin cans nailed to the floor to stop the ants and bugs. We got no running water. No electric. I can't do nothing like you suggest."

"Well, I'm afraid there is no alternative. I will have to amputate."

She shook her head. "But can't you keep her here? Treat her like you said?"

"Mrs McDonald, you can see this isn't a colored hospital. We are a charitable institution. We depend entirely on benefactors. I have a responsibility towards them, the other patients and the staff. It is out of the question that your daughter be treated here. We do what we can, of course. I am prepared to amputate the foot and discharge her tomorrow, but even that is beyond my remit. This is not a colored hospital. She should not be here at all."

"You gotta tell her, doctor. Please, you gotta tell her." The doctor gave a curt nod and returned to the ward with the mother, unusually subdued, trailing behind him.

As he approached the bed, he focused on the girl lying there. The infection in her body was pulsing through her veins, poisoning her, yet she still had a sparkle about her. In a ward crammed full with sick children, she was the one that stood out.

Not because she was the only black child, but because ... he couldn't put his finger on it, but she drew him in with her face, for no explicable reason.

His heart sank. It was hard to tell a child that he would have to cut part of her leg off, but it was better that than tell a mother she had lost a child. He sat down at the edge of the child's bed and began.

"Josephine, have you looked at your foot?" The child shook her head with the most serious of expressions on her face, but there was a cheekiness about her movements. The

doctor, to his surprise, found himself suppressing a smile. The child was most engaging. Not at all like her mother.

"Your foot, I'm sorry to say, is black and swollen. When you stood on the nail, it became infected and poison entered your system. The poison has spread, and now I will have to cut off the foot."

"No!" the child screeched as she grabbed hold of him and struggled to get out of bed. He felt the strength in her fingers as they dug into his arm. He was surprised because she was skinny, no doubt malnourished. Her soulful eyes gazed into his accusingly.

"I'm sorry. There really is no alternative. There's nowhere for you to recuperate. I can't look after you here. There are too many children who need treatment. I can't give you a hospital bed here indefinitely. I'm sure you understand that I can't gamble with your life."

"Doctor, please ..." She clung to him as she pleaded. "I'll die if I can't dance. I can't dance with no foot."

"I'm sorry, Josephine. There really is no alternative. We can operate this afternoon, and you can return to your home tomorrow."

He tried to stand up, but her fingers grasped his arm like the talons of an eagle, digging into his flesh with a tenacity that belied her age and stature.

"I will die," she said her eyes staring into his. The doctor stared back at the child. He could see she spoke the truth. He turned to look at the mother – she nodded solemnly.

His thoughts were in turmoil. A black child, in the ward for six to eight weeks. How could he justify that to the trustees, the staff, the other patients? Such an admission would put his whole career in jeopardy.

He had successfully resisted pressure to join the Ku Klux Klan, but he could not pretend to ignore their influence. Admitting this child into a white hospital for the length of time required to save her foot would stretch the trustees to the very limits of tolerance. If he lost this position, he would not be able to treat any black children. The few he had

admitted from time to time had been an indulgence which only his long service to the hospital afforded him. If he pushed too hard on the invisible

boundaries that surrounded him, he would forfeit his position and with it his ability to help the neediest of the black children.

While there were efforts underway to provide a colored hospital in St Louis, it would be years in coming. Too late for Josephine. Her foot, once amputated, would be gone for good and with it, if she and her mother were to be believed, any reason she had to live.

Mother and daughter looked at him intently, as if caught in the frame of a silent movie. Their lives were in his hands. What would he decide? His eyes trailed along the rows of beds: white children, born into poverty. Why else would they require treatment at the hospital? White staff accustomed to looking after white children. Staff entitled to refuse to administer to a black child. White patients entitled to be treated in a ward free of blacks, no matter how needy. In the balance, the desperate face of a child who didn't deserve to be there, driven into his care by poverty and a lack of shoes. What would he decide?

Time stood still as the doctor struggled to balance his wishes with the strict rules imposed by the hospital trustees. Finally, his decision.

He turned back to Josephine and taking her hand he said, "Very well, Josephine, we will try."

She threw her arms around his neck. "Thank you, thank you," she said effusively.

Her mother shook his hand vigorously as she too expressed her thanks.

"Mrs McDonald, let me walk you to the end of the ward" as he escorted her to the door. He explained the proposed treatment, which would involve drainage and frequent cleaning and changing of bandages. As he said goodbye to her, he added firmly, "No visitors. We will send word when the child may be collected."

Chapter 2

GRATIOT STREET, ST LOUIS, 1914

"What you gone and done now, girl?" Carrie McDonald boomed. Josephine stood at the door of their home. Head lowered. Beside her, Mrs. Mason. Josephine was wearing a pretty dress with patterns of red and yellow, leather shoes, which looked new, and white socks. Her hair was neatly pleated, and if pushed, Carrie would have admitted that she had looked twice at her daughter to make sure it was her. Having recognized Josephine, her focus turned to the brown paper parcel under her arm.

"I'm sorry, Mrs McDonald," the lady explained politely. "It isn't going to work out with Josephine, but she is welcome to keep her clothes and the spare set I bought for her.

I'll say good day to you." The lady nodded and began to walk away.

"But Mrs Mason, I'm sure we can work this out," Carrie said, barely halted by the shock of the lady's words. "I know she is a willful child, but she has a kind heart and she is a good worker." "I'm sorry", the lady said. "We really can't keep her." Carrie could have sworn there were tears in her eyes. But the lady walked away. She did not look back.

"But what you gone and done?" she asked angrily. "I done well finding you that place. Look she gone and got you all them nice, new clothes, and shoes," she added, the intonation on her voice rising. "When you had that before and what you gone and done to spoil it all? You know there ain't no room here for you, not with me, Arthur and your brother and sisters? What do you think we going to do now? We ain't got your wages no more. You the oldest. You got to think about your responsibilities to your brother and sisters."

"I didn't do nothing, Mama."

"Well, you sure gone and done something, or she would never have brought you back. You better tell me cos you'll get a good hiding if you don't tell the truth and if you done something you shouldn't have."

"I ain't done nothing. I done all she said I had to do. Why I got up at six in the morning and I cleaned the kitchen. I gathered coals. I laid the fires. Then at nine, I went to school just like we said. After school finished, I ironed and cleaned just like you told me."

"Why she gone and bring you back then if you done all she said?"

"I don't know, Mama. After I done all my chores, I thought she real happy with me. She say I can have my friends from school come over. Why I made a stage in the basement and I done plays. I dressed up like a princess from the East, just like in the books in school, and I dance and sing. I even charge those children a couple of pennies and they pay me, Mama. They come every afternoon, and one day I am a princess like in *Ali Baba* and another I'm a dancer like on the best stage in New York, and they love it, Mama. I got kids come and pay to watch me." The child's eyes lit up and her voice trembled with excitement.

"Well, hell, child, that's it. You been fooling around instead of working. No wonder you gone and lost your place there." Her voice was angry. Josephine ducked to avoid a slap still protesting her innocence.

"No, it weren't nothing to do with that. She gone and lent me her curtains and old dresses for my costumes. Sometimes she come and watch. She gone and laugh so much at my shows. She said, 'Child, you do my heart good. You is born for the stage.'"

"Well, she sure had a good reason to get rid of you, when she come here without so much as sending a note ahead. What you gonna say about that, girl? And it had better be good because I don't know where you gonna find another to take you in like that."

"It was the ghost, Mama. I was frightened of the ghost."

"What you talking about? You know fine well your ancestors were Indians who talk to the spirits and Negros who know black magic. What call you got to be scared of ghosts?"

"It wasn't no ghost like I seen before, Mama. It was as night it come. I had my own room with my own bed. With sheets and pillows and all. I was lying in my bed and I heard it. Coming from outside, noises louder and louder. Then tapping at my shutters. I got so scared that I screamed and screamed. Why I woke Mrs Mason up and she came running in my room and then she stayed with me until I fall asleep."

The child's eyes were wide as she recited the tale.

"And the same thing happened the next night and the next night. I was so scared, Mama. And Mrs Mason was so nice. Why she say she going to stay with me all night till we get to the bottom of it. She promised me that there ain't no such thing as ghosts. I guess she never heard of the spirits of the great plain," the child whispered. "Well, I was thankful she promised to stay with me, and she sat in a rocking chair by my bed. I so happy and so tired that I fall straight asleep. Why the next thing I know, Mr Mason is in bed beside me and Mrs Mason is screaming. Was her screams that woke me up. No ghost. She was plain angry with Mr Mason. She say he ain't got no right coming in my bedroom at night. He say he wanted to see that I was alright. Well, she got upset and say he got no place coming in my bed even if I is scared. She shouted at him some and he went to their room. The next day I didn't see him at all, but Mrs Mason say it's time for me to go home. And here I am. I didn't do nothing wrong, Mama. I swear."

Her mother laughed. "There's times, girl, I think you ain't got the wits you was born with. One thing's sure, you ain't gonna find another place like that one."

Chapter 3

ST LOUIS, 1916

The rain pitter-pattered against the cardboard. The noise softened as the paper dampened and became soggy. Josephine pulled the blanket more closely around her, huddling to shut out the cold, trying to stop shivering. A bellow of swearing shattered through the black night. Heart thumping, Josephine shrunk into her wet shelter. It was the tramp who had dossed down next to her. Judging by the words, his booze had run dry. She started when she heard glass splintering. Her fingers gripped the coins she had earned from street dancing – enough to eat tomorrow, but not enough for a doss-house tonight. Stretching her limbs, she prepared to run. She had learned the hard way how to survive the city at night.

She heard the man shuffle off in the other direction. She was safe – for now. Alert for more signs of danger, she was determined not to cry. One of her younger sisters, Willie May, had come to find her today. "Please, come home," she had begged. "Mama says you can – there's always a place for you."

But Josephine couldn't go back. Not the way things were. The last time she had been home, the lines had been drawn. There was no changing what had been said. It was a question that burned through every part of her. Her mother refused to understand.

She stood out. She was black, but not as black as her mother and brother and sisters.

She had heard snippets of gossip filtered here and there from sources she could no longer remember, whispers, laughter behind her back, teasing and ridicule at school.

Why had her mama been confined in a white only hospital for her birth when her brother and sisters had been born at home, like all the other children at her school?

Why had her mama been allowed to stay in a white hospital for six weeks? Unimaginable for a black domestic. And even more mysterious, who had paid for it? Not Eddie Carson, who she was supposed to believe was her father. Not her mama. Who then? And if it was her mother's employers who had paid, why should it be such a secret if it was a genuine act of benevolence? Memories of her most recent quarrel with her mother ran through her head like a flickering newsreel on constant repeat.

"I have a right to know who my real father is?"

"Eddie Carson is the only father you ever gonna have. Don't you ever think otherwise."

"He can't be my father."

"I ain't got nothing to say, girl."

"Mama, the kids at school tease me. Look at me," she had yelled, fighting back tears as she held up her arms. "I ain't the same color as you, Eddie Carson or either my brother or sisters. Everyone says my father is white. Tell me, Mama."

"You ain't got no white father. Don't you ever go thinking that, girl. You just bring trouble on us all with that kinda talk." Carrie struck Josephine on the face. As her daughter reeled from the blow Carrie raged, "Don't you go forgetting they lynch women same as men. Don't you ever go thinking you got a white father."

"I can't stay here if you won't tell me the truth."

"Where you gonna go, girl? I ain't got nothing to tell you." Her mother had taken her firmly by the shoulders and shaken her. "You gotta promise me you gonna stop this talk. You ain't got no white father."

Chapter 4

BOX TOWN, ST LOUIS, 2 JULY 1917

"Get up!" yelled her mama. Josephine pulled the blanket more closely around her and snuggled into her sister. It was the middle of the night. Rough hands gripped her shoulder.

"Now!"

Less drowsy this time, Josephine could hear screams and yelling. Opening her eyes, she could see terror in her mother's face.

Gunshots. Loud. Close. Getting closer.

Josephine felt scared. Scared like she had never felt before. She joined her mother in forcing her brother and sisters out of the bed they all shared.

"Run," her mother screamed as a burning torch crashed through the window. Josephine glanced back as they fled into the darkness. Flames licked round the boxcar they had called home. The tin cans they had hammered between the cracks in the floorboards to stop the rats crawling into the house were no defense against the flames now climbing up the walls.

Josephine ran back to save one of her puppies that had escaped from her grip. Outlined against the flames she saw a wailing baby tossed into the air. A shot rang out. The baby's cries stopped. Gulping back the bile that rose from her stomach, she turned, searching for her family. They were gone. Disappeared into the chaos. She stood transfixed trying to decide where to run. The sounds around her were deafening.

Gunshots. Screams. Breaking glass. The acrid smoke choked her lungs, and she could smell burning. Burning wood. Burning flesh. She wanted to vomit but couldn't. She was too scared to move.

"Don't struggle," a voice said. "I'll get you across the river."

She felt arms around her, picking her up. She gripped tightly to her pets. The stranger carried her over the East Saint bridge to St Louis. To safety. Josephine snuggled into the little dogs. They were safe – for now.

The next day, Josephine walked along the river banks. The stench of death made the bile rise from her stomach. She hadn't eaten. There was nothing to eat, but she felt like she could never eat again. Not after everything she had seen. She stopped, shrinking back in fear as she saw two officials drag a corpse from the river. They covered the body immediately, but not before she had seen it had no arms.

Chapter 5

ST LOUIS, 1919

"Mama, Mama. You got to go talk to Josephine." Tears were pouring down Willie May's face, leaving tracks where the particles of grime had attached. Her eyes were swollen and red.

Carrie McDonald put down the iron and carefully placed it on the table.

"Calm down. Tell me what's wrong?"

"She's stopped knitting."

Carrie looked at her daughter, puzzled.

"She said there's no baby. Weren't ever no baby."

"Where is she?"

"She's at home. She won't talk. Won't say nothing. Nothing except that there weren't ever no baby."

Her mother jumped into action, handing the iron to her daughter. "You finish. It's to be delivered by six pm." Barely stopping to grab her bag, she left the laundry with its sign beside the door: WE WASH FOR WHITE CUSTOMERS ONLY.

"What's happened?" Carrie demanded as she walked into the room that Josephine and her husband had moved into. Josephine was scrubbing the floor. "Ain't nothing happened," the girl answered without looking up.

Carrie's eyes darted around the room. The neatly folded freshly knitted baby clothes were gone from their place under the bed. The knitting pins and wool were no longer in the basket beside the stove. Even the picture of Josephine and her husband had disappeared.

"Where's them baby clothes you were making?"

"Weren't ever no baby clothes."

"I saw them, Josephine. With my own eyes. You tell me what's happened."

"Ain't nothing happened, Mama."

"Tell me, please. The baby ..."

"Ain't no baby. Ain't gonna be no baby."

"Josephine, where's Willie?"

"He gone, Mama. He ain't coming back."

Carrie leaned in to touch her daughter, who quickly pulled away. It was then that Carrie noticed the bruising under her left eye. "Stop that." Carrie stood squarely on the floor Josephine was trying to scrub. "Talk to me."

"Ain't got the time right now. Got this to finish."

"You seen a doctor, girl? Why I got the money here." Carrie reached into her bag and produced a few coins, which she held out towards her daughter.

"Ain't got no need of no doctor, Mama."

"Josephine, you young. You still only thirteen. It ain't unusual to lose the first. Why Mrs Hanson lost her first two and now she got three all fit as fiddles."

"Ain't lost nothing."

"You need to get checked out, girl, just to be sure."

"Ain't got no need of a doctor. You gotta go now, Mama. I got work to do." Josephine stood up, walked over to the door and opened it.

"Please, Josephine." Carrie stepped towards her daughter and grabbed her arm.

As she did so, Josephine shook free and yelled angrily, "I mean it, Mama, you gotta go now."

Carrie stepped back, alarmed by the ferocity in her daughter's voice. She was only thirteen, but she had the force of a grown woman. Carrie paused as she saw the pain in Josephine's eyes, spiraling all the way to her soul.

"Don't keep this bottled up. Grieve, child. There will be another baby."

"Get out, Mama. I've been nice, but now you got to go. I ain't got nothing to say."

"You can't keep this locked up inside you. You gotta let it out. Otherwise, you gonna carry this pain your whole life."

Chapter 6

ST LOUIS 1919

Tears rolled down her Margaret's face, unchecked, like a salty river, splashing onto her dress, spotting and darkening the light cotton fabric.

Josephine watched unmoved. Arms crossed.

"Please don't go.," Margaret wailed. "I gotta tell Ma. You can't just go like this." She made as if to grab the carpet bag Josephine had packed with her few possessions.

Josephine erupted into action. Grabbing her sister's shoulders and shaking her. "Don't you dare tell. You promised me."

"But..." Margaret tried to interrupt, sniffing.

"I can't tell her. You know she'll try to stop me. And I ain't gonna let her. Ain't no-one going to stop me."

Josephine's eyes flashed with anger. She looked round the bedroom she shared with her sisters. The clapboard walls and the knotted wooden floor. The solitary chair beside the bed. It was barely more comfortable than she imagined a prison cell to be. Tonight would be her last night there, ever. She was close now. To grabbing her future. She could sense it deep in her heart. No-one would stand in her way. Not her mother, not her stepfather, not even Margaret.

Her sister calmed as she realised there was no changing

Josephine's mind with threats. She wiped the tears from her face as she made one final attempt at persuasion.

"Mama would understand. You know how she talks about when she was on the stage. When she was young. How she loved it."

She wouldn't let me go. You know she wouldn't. She'd say like she always does, "what you think you got that I didn't have? And what good did it do me all that dancing and

singing and travelling? I still ended up buried under a pile of linen. Washing for whites. That's where you'll end up. Same as me." Josephine mimicked their mother perfectly.

Margaret stared at Josephine, her eyes widening as the implications of her sister's words took hold.

"'How many times you heard her say them very words? She ain't gonna let me go.

And, hell, Margaret, I can't stay here."

Josephine paused. How could she explain the fire that burned in her very soul? Hell, a fire? It weren't no fire, it was a furnace. That raged and burned. She knew once she got on the train in the morning with the Dixie Steppers she was going. She weren't quite sure where but she was going. And she wasn't going to stop. And she wasn't going to look back. Not ever.

Chapter 7

THE PLANTATION CLUB NEW YORK 1925

"Hey Jo, there's a lady here to see you."

Josephine laughed. "Makes a change," she joked, winking at the waiter as she turned towards the dressing room. "Who is she?"

"Caroline Dudley Reagan."

"Never heard of her. Tell her to leave a card." Josephine wasn't even curious. She tired of the attention, male and female, which had not abated although she was Mrs Josephine Baker now, albeit estranged from her adoring and patient spouse.

"She says its urgent. She needs to speak to you. Lives in Paris, apparently. Her husband works at the American Embassy there."

Josephine sighed. This woman appeared to have impressed the waiter, but she had better things to do.

"It sounds really important," he confided. "She says she has an offer for you."

"That sounds more interesting. Tell her to come back here."

She peered through the curtains towards the round tables with their white starched tablecloths, circling the dancefloor. An elegant woman rose to her feet in response to the tuxedoed waiter's signal. Josephine watched, her sense of intrigue growing. The lady did not seem typical of the club's usually frivolous clientele. Everything about her manner signaled "purpose."

"Josephine," the woman gushed. "I'm so pleased to finally meet you. I'm Caroline Dudley Reagan. I loved your performance. You make the show."

Josephine glanced around. That kind of talk did not make her popular with the other chorus girls.

Caroline asked, "Isn't there somewhere we can talk more privately?"

Josephine shrugged. She couldn't go out front with the audience and backstage was by definition a crazy microcosm of Harlem life.

Josephine noticed the manager's office was empty. 'We could talk here for a moment," she suggested. Caroline followed her and Josephine closed the door.

"You have an offer?"

"Yes, let me explain. I want you to come to Paris with me?"

"Paris?" Josephine asked, not completely sure where that was.

"France. Europe."

All Josephine heard, was "far."

"I'm forming a troupe to perform a show called *The Revue Négre*. I have seen your reviews from *Shuffle Along* and *Chocolate Dandies*. You're perfect for a comedy part. There'll be twenty-five performers in total. You'd be paid two hundred and fifty dollars a week. That's more than you get here, surely?"

Josephine nodded, but her heart was saying "*no*." As long as she was in New York there was always a possibility of a reconciliation with Willie, if she decided that was what she wanted, but France! All the way across the ocean!

Caroline continued as if she hadn't noticed her reluctance. "I want to take jazz to Europe. Imagine," Caroline enthused, "they've never experienced its magic there. They don't know how to dance the Charleston." Josephine was already feeling sorry for these Europeans that had never shifted and shimmied to the strains of a jazz orchestra. Who'd never had their heartstrings tugged by the sound of a lone sax. Who'd never experienced the thrill of a night out in Harlem.

But Europe. That was far. How'd she ever get back? She began to shake her head.

"There's no segregation there." Caroline continued. "Liberty, Equality, Fraternity, that's what the French believe. "

"Now this lady's talking," Josephine thought, beginning to smile.

Chapter 8

SS BERENGARIA, 16 SEPTEMBER 1925

The ship stretched along the harbor, a mighty black island. Her three funnels belched smoke, and along her decks, uniformed figures moved incessantly like tiny white ants. Instructions were yelled over the noise of the throng who packed the quays. Goods swung precariously over the decks from cranes as they were lowered into the hull.

Josephine froze, suddenly struck by the enormity of what she was about to do. Now was the moment. Could she really leave her homeland? Could she really set sail on this terrifying ship for Paris, France? A country where she knew no one. Where she could not even speak the language. The gangplank stretched before her like a pathway either to a whole new world or a disaster off an enormity she could not even imagine. Caroline slipped her hand through her arm. "Don't worry, we'll walk up together."

Josephine took a deep breath and smiled, although she was terrified. As they reached the ship, they were greeted by the steward.

"Welcome," he bowed. "Let me show you to your quarters," he said, obviously speaking to Caroline. Josephine's confidence plummeted as she noticed the sign behind the steward to which he had alluded by movement without actually saying anything.

It read: COLOREDS. And it had an arrow beneath pointing no doubt in the direction of steerage.

Josephine sighed. Why was she surprised? Had she not seen the American flag flying from the ship's stern? She might be sailing away from the racial prejudice that blighted her life, but the racial prejudice was clearly sailing with her and was set to be her travel companion.

She could not follow Caroline to the first-class section. Instead she had to make her way to steerage with the rest of the dance troupe. No private cabins with running water for them. They were housed in a large compartment with rows of beds and little in the way of comforts. As they explored, they discovered that as "coloreds" they were excluded from certain parts of the ship.

It appeared there would be little opportunity to liaise with Caroline regarding the forthcoming Paris performance, so Josephine could not contain her excitement when a note arrived for her from Caroline. She had been invited to perform a set as part of the onboard entertainment program. She was going to make first class after all.

The days passed slowly for Josephine. The Atlantic Ocean stretched ahead, cold and grey as they sped onwards to her future.

The ship's klaxon sounded to indicate a lifeboat drill. Routine, the crew muttered, but there had been a lifeboat drill the day before. The more experienced transatlantic passengers commented that there was usually only one drill per crossing.

Josephine, glancing upwards, could see the first-class passengers on their deck lining up beside the boats. There was a tenseness in the expressions of the crew that had not been present on the previous exercise. Why did they appear to be searching the ship? That hadn't happened yesterday, and didn't this drill seem to be taking considerably longer than the last one? She could hear some of the children begin to cry and passengers begin to complain about the inconvenience. She and the rest of the passengers on her lower deck had not yet been issued with lifejackets, and she watched with sadness as the crew worked their way down from first class to second class to third class and finally to steerage. The saving of life was clearly prioritized according to the price of a ticket, and hers was the cheapest. She pushed her way towards one of the crew men who was delving into the deck storage trunks. She rolled her eyes and asked, "What's going on?"

"It's a standard drill," he replied without interrupting his activity. She grabbed his arm and swung him towards her. She rolled her eyes again and put on a goofy expression.

He couldn't help but laugh.

"What's really going on?"

He glanced to either side. "Look, we can't afford a panic. Here," he said, pushing a lifejacket towards her. "Take this, and stand on the deck nearest the sea, beside one of the boats. That's the safest place to be."

"Tell me what's going on or I'll cause one humdinger of a scene."

"You promise not to tell anyone else?"

She nodded. It seemed the quickest way of getting the information.

"There was a letter handed in at the Cunard office in New York claiming there's a bomb on the ship and that it's scheduled to explode," he glanced at his watch, "just about now."

Josephine stepped back in shock.

"We're sure it's a hoax," he said. "Don't worry. We have to carry out our procedures. You will be able to go back inside in a few minutes."

Chapter 9

STUDIO PAUL COLIN, PARIS, OCTOBER 1925

He looked at her curiously, then after a brief pause, ran his finger along her jawline.

"You are perfect," he said in a dispassionate way, as if she were a statue in a museum, not flesh and blood, living and breathing with thoughts and feelings of her own.

"You should get undressed," he said. "Then sit over there." He gestured to a chair positioned between two pillars, with a draped red velvet backdrop.

"But I can't," she said. This wasn't what she had agreed to. He looked at her more closely. Her eyes were still bloodshot, and she cast them downwards, but too late.

"You've been crying," he said. Again, his voice was distant, unimpassioned, like a judge with no preconceptions. A judge who was uninterested in social niceties or middle-class morals. Josephine felt immediately that she could seek his advice. She realized he would not judge for judgement's sake.

"I don't know what to do," she explained.

He shrugged.

"They've said I have to dance naked. Naked, except for a pink feather between my legs. I don't know what to do. I have no money.

No way of getting back to America. Why I can barely speak a word of French."

"But you can learn, my dear," he said, as though she had not shocked him.

"Did you hear me?"

He could hear the tears, even though they were not running down her cheeks.

"But of course they do. What else?"

Her eyes were wide when she returned his gaze, shocked by his reaction.

"Such beauty, your limbs ... your body when it moves ... it is art," he whispered as he took her hand and led her to the prepared set. "Can't you see?" He gestured to a mirror positioned to the side. "You are so beautiful. It would be a crime to keep yourself covered. Look at yourself. Feast! Do what they ask, Josephine."

She hesitated but continued to listen.

"I have been commissioned to prepare the posters for the forth-coming performance of *La Revue Negre*. When I saw you at the rehearsals, I insisted that you be my model. You will be the star of the show. I will make sure of that."

Chapter 10

MONTPARNASSE, PARIS, MAY 1926

She sipped the café crème enjoying the rush of caffeine. Tucked in a corner, peeking out onto the boulevard, she relaxed as she watched the Paris scene playing before her. All of life paraded past, just for her entertainment. A young couple strolled along the street, a black soldier in a French army uniform and a chic flapper who swayed elegantly by his side despite her high heels and the cobbled street. They paused for a moment, kissing as if they were in love and it was the most natural thing in the world. Josephine couldn't take her eyes off them. They had no idea – but why should they – that where she came from their actions would result in the woman being flogged, at the very least, and ostracized, and the man being lynched and tortured by an angry white mob. How she loved Paris. Just being free to walk down the street without having to worry if she was breaking one colored law or another was enough to make her feel drunk on freedom. It was a heady brew as intoxicating as any alcohol. She chuckled to herself. She was addicted to freedom. No drink or drug could ever make her feel like she did in Paris. The city of light, with its brightness, had dissolved all the layers of discrimination that had stifled her when she lived in America. Josephine tapped her shoe on the floor to the time of the strains of a jazz trombone, a skilled player, probably another of her compatriots who had fled the discrimination in America and come to Paris to experience the unbridled hedonism of the city. She waved to a couple of her fellow dancers who looked as if they were heading home for some shut-eye before the evening performance. She knew she should probably get her head down for an hour or two, but she hated to sleep for a moment longer than absolutely necessary. There was too much to do, to see, to experience. She couldn't bear to waste a second of it.

It was Tuesday, so soon she would go to La Coupole, Montparnasse where the English-speaking writers Ernest Hemingway and F. Scott Fitzgerald met. She would pass an hour or two with them, then later in the evening, the band would begin to play. Raucous jazz would blare as a seething mass of bodies shook and shimmied as if life itself depended

upon it. Men and women, scantily dressed, would hoist themselves up and cling to the elegant columns of the café. The best and the worst of the avant-garde would be there, along with the youth who had escaped alive from the destruction of war. Josephine would slip away for her own performance at *Revue Negre*, return to the café or maybe go to a party, then after a few hours of sleep, it would be time to do it all again. The only change would be the café she attended and the company she kept. Perhaps she'd go to the one with the French writers and spend time with Georges Simenon and his friends, or the one with Salvador Dali and other Spanish artists. She might go for a driving lesson, and then it would be the weekend when the whole Paris scene would explode into a crazy party where the only rule, as Cole Porter so clearly advocated, was "Anything Goes." How she loved Paris. How she loved life.

Chapter 11

PARIS EVENING GAZETTE

CHEZ JOSEPHINE

It was with considerable pleasure I was able to accept an invitation to Chez Josephine as the nightclub opened its doors for the first time. Situated on Rue Fontaine in Montmartre, the club is perfectly situated for Harlem on the Seine.

The menu is a combination of soul food and cordon bleu cuisine with an eclectic roster of performances. The guests present suggest that Chez Josephine is poised to become a modernist salon for the Paris avant-garde.

As midnight approached, the atmosphere in the club intensified. A feeling of suspense hung in the air, increasingly unbearable with each tick of the clock. Finally, just after midnight La Baker arrived. She appeared resplendent in a silver gown skimming over her body and flowing down over endless legs. She wore a magnificent diamond necklace with a matching tiara. Her presence was extraordinary. Silence swept over the room as those gathered enjoyed a moment's silence to behold her beauty.

The Black Venus wandered around the room like a queen greeting her subjects, holding out a hand to be kissed, a nod of acknowledgement. No one could fail to be enthralled by her charisma, her beauty, her gracefulness. Is it any wonder she has received thousands of love letters and marriage proposals? What man with blood in his veins could fail to be entranced by her charms?

Ms Baker has a grueling schedule of performances at Folies Bergère and arrived at Chez Josephine directly after her performance there. If she was tired, it did not show. Indeed, La Baker gave every indication of being ready to dance all night.

She took to the stage with one lucky customer to provide a very public Charleston lesson, and then she sang a couple of numbers. The intimate setting of her club and the opportunity to be so close to such an incredible star make an evening at Chez Josephine unmissable.

With so many famous customers in the audience, it is also an opportunity to rub shoulders with the great and the good of Paris society. I predict Chez Josephine will soon become a mandatory experience for visitors to our city. I have seen Paris and spent an evening at Chez Josephine. I shall die happy!

Chapter 12

BERLIN, 13 FEBRUARY 1927

"Come."

Cosette stared at Josephine, feeling like a mouse caught in the mesmerizing gaze of a playful cat. It was difficult to say no, but she already had plans.

"I'm sorry, but I've promised to meet Sammy." She blushed and added confidentially, "I really like him, and we don't get many chances to meet up."

Josephine rolled her eyes, laughing and shaking her head.

"You must come with me. This is important. You're going to meet Max Reinhart, the great director. You know what he can do for your career. You don't want to be a chorus girl for the rest of your life, do you? If he takes a liking to you, you'll be a star."

Cosette shook her head. "Don't go teasing me. You know it's only you that he's interested in."

"Listen, Cosette." Josephine grasped her arm and stared intently at her. "Do you think I just got to be the most famous girl in the world by turning down opportunities? I left my husband because I needed to be on the stage. I'm a dancer. I loved him, my Willie Baker, but he couldn't make my soul feel like how it does when I dance. There ain't no man alive can make me feel like that. And I think you're the same.

I just got this feeling. Why Mr Reinhart invited me this evening, and he told me to bring another girl to dance. I thought about you right away. I thought if I have to take another girl along then it's got to be you."

"But Sammy"

''Sammy's gonna be here tomorrow. But Mr Reinhart

won't be. He's the director of the Deutsches Theatre, and he wants to give me a three-year contract. After that, he promised I will be the greatest star in Europe. Think of what he could do for you, Cosette."

Josephine stretched out. She wasn't wearing much, just a spangled bra and a string. She strolled in front of Cosette, her movements slow, controlled, exuding sexuality and an animal magnetism. Cosette was transfixed, as she was every night by Josephine's performance. By her presence. Her movements demanded her audience's absolute attention, as though there was nothing else.

Josephine twirled round. Holding out a pen and pad to Cosette, she instructed, "Write a note. Say you're indisposed and will meet him tomorrow. Sammy doesn't pay your bills, does he? A girl has to look after herself in this world. Reinhart can make you a star. Imagine, Sammy and a hundred others like him will be at your feet every night if it's your name in lights.

Reinhart can do that for you. He asked me to bring someone and it's you I want."

Cosette bit her lip as she thought about the opportunity awaiting.

"What you got to lose? Sammy don't need to know nothing about tonight. I ain't gonna tell him."

Josephine had such force. Such charisma. She seemed to fill every room she walked into. Cosette wanted to be like her. She wanted to have the world at her fingertips. She took the pen and scribbled the note.

"Hurry, grab your things. The car's waiting."

Cosette could never have imagined any house as grand as the Reinhart mansion. She had certainly never seen one like it. As they climbed the steps to the front door, the door glided open before they even had a chance to knock.

Josephine, now wearing a long fur, swept through. She was accustomed to being treated like royalty, but for Cosette, it was nerve-wracking and new.

But every fiber in her body tingled. She had never felt important before and she was enjoying the attention, even if it was deflected from Josephine.

They were shown to a large reception room where men in black tuxedos sipped champagne while waiters tended their needs with deference bordering on slavery. Cosette shrunk behind Josephine whispering, "We're the only women here."

Josephine, eyes flashing, quipped, "Of course there are no other women. Why would there be? We are here." She then stretched out her arms and a servant lifted her fur coat from her shoulders revealing that she was naked apart from a pink loincloth.

Cosette first felt alarmed, then exhilarated as the men flocked around Josephine. Then envious as she played moon to Josephine's blazing sun. But it awakened her desire, her ambition. She knew only too well that Josephine had risen from the most desperate of circumstances to be one of the most celebrated women in the world, never mind France. Cosette would be content with a fraction of the success of her companion. She wondered if this evening really was the first step on a road that would guarantee her fame and fortune.

She smiled rapturously at the assembled men and tried to emulate Josephine's confidence, movements and gestures. Had she not been selected personally by Josephine from all the other chorus girls? Did this not mean that she had every reason to expect that she could aspire to a meteoric rise to fame similar to that of her mentor?

Cosette was ready. She wanted it. The success she craved was at her fingertips, if only she had the strength and will to grab it.

Josephine's derriere swayed as she moved panther-like around the room, greeting the men she knew with a flamboyant kiss to each cheek and holding out her hand to be kissed by the others she was introduced to.

Cosette watched jealously as Josephine drew all the attention. Her presence was as compelling as a drug.

She wanted to have that effect too. Was she not a dancer every bit as accomplished as Josephine?

Having toured the room, Josephine passed her a flute of champagne as she sipped her own. "Come on. They're going to get impatient if they have to wait any longer for the entertainment." Josephine winked as she signaled a waiter to put on a record. Josephine led her to the silver bowl containing cocaine which was discreetly placed at a side door. "Take some."

"No, really, I don't want to."

"Don't be silly, everyone is having some.".

Cosette dared not disobey.

"Come on," Josephine pulled her into the center of the room. She could feel the intense gaze upon them. She knew in her heart it was Josephine who commanded the attention of everyone else there, but standing beside her, she could feel the deflected rays of adoration, of captivation, of pure uninhibited lust – it was as intoxicating as the drug she had just snorted..

The lively steps of the Charleston flooded the room as the record player burst into life. Josephine flashed her smile and immediately her body took on a life of its own, as if she was possessed by the music. Cosette followed the movements, matching Josephine as best she could, knowing in her heart that she could never hope to achieve the same flexibility and fluidity of movement.

As the number ended, Josephine signaled a record change and then grabbed Cosette in a sultry tango-esque number. She was not familiar with this style of music and felt lost not knowing what steps to take, but Josephine grabbed her hand and pulled her close.

"Look at them," she whispered in her ear. Cosette glanced at the men. They watched the dance as if transfixed. "Let's give them what they want – the performance of their life. They will remember this night forever." Josephine's voice was husky, sexy, compelling.

Cosette felt overwhelmed by everything. The music. The madness. The intensity of their audience. The nakedness

of Josephine's body so close to her own. So intimate. So sexual. So intoxicating. Josephine led and they danced the tango. Slowly, intimately, as if no one was watching. As they moved, Josephine whispered directions.

Gradually, the room and their surroundings slipped away, leaving only their bare bodies touching and the music. When Josephine grasped her breast firmly, clasping the flesh between her elegant fingers, Cosette felt as if she had been waiting for that moment all of her life.

When Josephine wrapped her arms around her and slipped her hands over her buttocks, she moaned in raw pleasure. When Josephine's lips touched her skin, her body thrilled with excitement. She forgot they were being watched. There was only the moment and her body's need for satisfaction.

Chapter 13

PARIS, 3 JUNE 1927

"We can't!" Josephine exclaimed.

"We can, of course, we can." Pepito assured her and took her hand in his. "You just have to believe."

"But it's impossible."

"No," he overcame her resistance. "Do you think I was always a count? I dress like a count. I look like a count. I behave like a count. And when I came to Paris, I became a count."

Josephine regarded him. What he said was true. With his elegant mustache, elaborate gestures and stylish suits, he behaved and appeared just as everyone might imagine an Italian count would.

"You are ready now. You have transformed."

"I would hope so," she retorted. "All those lessons: ballet, singing, elocution, French, comportment. Why I barely have time to have fun anymore."

Pepito raised an eyebrow. No matter how exhausting her schedule, he knew that Josephine, with her endless stream of energy, always found time to play.

He continued, "We are on the way now. Your book will be published soon, and the film is underway. I have many other projects too, which will develop your career and ensure your continued success."

"You do want to be a countess, don't you?"

She leaned back in her chair considering his words. The ridiculousness of her having a title appealed enormously. Having made the decision, she didn't want to wait.

"Let's do it then. Let's announce we are married."

Pepito raised his hands in surprise. "But arrangements ... a wedding ... it will take some planning."

"No," she wrapped her hands around him and kissed him. "I can't wait. It has to be today. I will make an announcement to the press that we are married. Then I will be a countess *today*."

Chapter 14
PARIS, 1928

The doorman signaled a thumbs-up, ending the anxious lull which had fallen backstage. Once again, there was bustle and movements everywhere. Shouts in American and French. Girls flounced past in lavish costumes, their breasts naked, their high heels clicking on the floorboards.

"Let's get this show on the road," the manager shouted, and then the orchestra burst into life.

An expectant hush fell over the audience as the lights dimmed.

Josephine had just burst through the stage door. Energy swirled around her like a tornado. Shedding clothing as she moved, first a glove, then her coat, then her blouse slipping from her shoulders. She was virtually naked by the time she arrived at her dressing room, her dresser trailing behind her, picking up the discarded clothing.

The manager held out his hand, tapping his watch with a stern expression. Josephine flashed a smile and tossed her hand as if such things did not matter.

As she slipped on her string, she glanced the telegram beside her mirror. Picking it up, she paused, then ripped it open. She didn't hear the manager's three-minute call.

Josephine picked up an empty bottle of champagne and threw it at the mirror. Her reflection shattered along with it. As had her little sister's life. The money she had sent for her family and Willie May's schooling had not been enough to save her. Tears poured down her cheeks and she flung herself onto the daybed, hammering it with her fists, sobs contorting her body. Her sister had died at the hands of a back-street abortionist ridding her of the one thing she herself craved most in the world. The one thing no amount of money could ever buy.

The manager stormed into the dressing room. Picking up the telegram, he read: WILLIE MAY DEAD – COMPLICATIONS ABORTION.

Chapter 15

BERLIN, 1928

"Black devil! Black devil!" the mob shouted over and over again. Josephine covered her ears, trying to cut out the sound as she prayed for the train to leave. The guard's whistle shrilled, and after what seemed like a lifetime, the train finally pulled out of the station.

She dared to glance out the window and regretted it immediately. Men with their faces contorted with hate hammered their fists in the air as they yelled their slogan with one voice. Some held banners. All were wearing a Nazi armband and what appeared to be a form of uniform. "Brown shirts" she had been told. Night after night, they had come to her performances to disrupt the audience. Josephine couldn't understand why they hated her so. But she was frightened. As frightened as she had ever been in her life.

PART II

SOLDIER

SPY

Chapter 1
1 SEPTEMBER 1939

4.45 am Germany invades Poland without declaration of war.

6.00 am Bombardment of Warsaw begins. Fourteen of Poland's air bases are bombed rendering them unusable.

8.00 am The French President is informed of the attack and calls an urgent cabinet meeting.

The British Prime Minister, Neville Chamberlain, arranges an urgent cabinet meeting.

10.00 am Hitler announces that the Polish port of Danzig has been annexed into the German Empire.

5.00 pm in Paris, notices of mobilization appear in the streets.

2 SEPTEMBER

9.30 pm Britain sends a message to Germany calling for suspension of all aggressive acts against Poland.

10.00 pm France sends a message to Germany calling for suspension of all aggressive acts against Poland.

10.00 am Benito Mussolini, the Italian dictator, calls for a conference to try to avoid war. Britain and France agree, provided German troops withdraw to behind the Polish border.

8.30 pm Mussolini refuses to transmit the terms of the proposed conference to Germany.

Chapter 2

PARIS, 2 SEPTEMBER 1939

The city was not as he had left her. A lone cellist still played at the corner of Metropole, the strains of his music traveling mournfully along the tiled underground corridors of the Metro, but today no one stopped to dance. The men who filled the tunnels were no longer predominately wearing black suits and crisp white starched shirts; they were not the office workers and functionaries who kept the administrative wheels of Paris turning or the waiters and bartenders who manned the cafés and bistros. A river of hastily mobilized soldiers clogged the tunnels, swamping them with the muddy brown of their uniforms and drowning even the vivid reds and florals of the elegant ladies, carrying brightly colored handbags, which disguised their gas mask holders.

The women who shopped in Paris's select couturiers and sipped cafés in the bistros along the Champs Elysees had the clicks of their heels infused with the boisterous voices of the young men called to arms for the first time. On their way east to the Maginot Line, France's defensive boundary with Germany. Each commuter's face wore the same expression: anxious, intent, unsmiling. Each citizen hurried to their destination: home, bistro, work, where they would listen to a radio and the impending announcement from which would discern their fate.

He blinked as he emerged into the sunlight on the Avenue de la Motte Picquet. The streets too were changing even as he walked along the boulevard, for all the world was like a stage, where, between the set changes, an ambivalent stage hand had either forgotten or not bothered to draw the curtains.

Concierges, uniform in their pinafores, climbed precariously on steps or chairs to hammer hastily painted signs above stairways to the basements and cellars of their tenements: ABRI. Shelter, in preparation for the bombing raids, which would surely follow a proclamation of war. Windows were already being painted blue for the blackout and latticed with tape to prevent dangerous splintering. Protective measures, no doubt reassuring for the good citizens of Paris, but completely ineffective in the event of a direct hit from one of Hitler's bombs. Jacques Abtey felt a thrill of excitement. It was happening. Finally, he was being given the opportunity he had secretly craved, the chance to prove himself. In his pocket, the telegram: COME IMMEDIATELY IF YOU ARE STILL INTER-ESTED! VACANCY. PARIS. He stood outside the wrought iron gates of the prestigious École Militaire, the academy which boasted Napoléon amongst its former pupils. The magnificent façade of the Louis XV building with its domed center formed merely a backdrop to events within the courtyard itself. Today the grounds were filled with troops, dressed for war, trench coats buttoned, bullet belts slung across their shoulders, rifles with bayonets fixed, battle-ready. Their boots stamped on the paved courtyard. A brass band played. These were the best trained soldiers in Europe. The elite of the French army. They marched in ordered beauty. Line after line of men turning in unison, with the precision of an intricate machine, at barked commands. As the mobilization of troops continued, Jacques turned away and began to walk through the Parc du Champ-de-Mars. France might boast the greatest army in Europe, but he was closing that door behind him. He was about to enter a much more shadowy world. It was 2.00 pm when Captain Abtey arrived at Avenue de Tourville. The street was like any other in the district. Number two was unimposing. The entrance was identical to other residences in the street, stone steps with wrought iron railings lining either side climbed towards a solid black door. There was no polished brass sign on the outside as one might expect of a military office or even a private residence.

Jacques checked his telegram and glanced again at the street sign. It was the correct address. He knocked. The door swung open immediately. A muscular doorman checked his identity papers thoroughly before pointing him towards a reception desk where a polite and efficient matron indicated a chair where he could wait. Men with military bearing but dressed in civilian clothing walked purposefully past. Secretaries clicked through the hallway, in their heels carrying manila folders with CONFIDENTIAL stamped in red across the covers. While nothing seemed particularly out of the ordinary, Jacques was acutely aware that he was entering another world. Discarding all the traditional trappings of a military organization, the Deuxième Bureau was something darker and infinitely more mysterious.

A young man arrived. "Captain Abtey, this way. Lieutenant Colonel Schlesser will see you now." He was shown into an office, spartan and military in appearance.

"Welcome, Jacques," the Colonel stood up as Jacques entered. and shook hands before gesturing him to a plain wooden chair in front of his desk. The Colonel, a tall, slim, imposing man, was dressed not in uniform but in a well-cut suit with waistcoat and cravat. Jacques caught the faint whiff of aftershave, which hinted at a mysterious oriental origin. "Excellent to have you join us. This is Captain Paillole," the Colonel continued. "Jacques helped us out with a suspect in thirty-six and expressed an interest in joining us here. I messaged him yesterday to come immediately if he was still interested and voilà." Jacques shook hands with the newcomer who took his place in the remaining vacant chair. "I want us to be clear about your roles in the future. We, here at the Deuxième Bureau, occupy a very sensitive diplomatic position. The address even of this building is classified information. No one, outside the highest government echelons of power, knows of our existence. We are so secret the government will never acknowledge us if we are compromised. Gentlemen, this is a bureau which does not exist. I must warn you that this has some rather unpleasant consequences. The first is the Geneva Conventions. For us, they have no application. Our department does not exist. We have no uniform to shield us from an enemy firing squad. No diplomatic immunity. The second more mundane consequence is that our budget, unsurprisingly for a department which does not exist, is meagre. Third, our jurisdiction is a murky swamp. Officially, it is the Sûreté who police Paris, we have no authority here. Our jurisdiction lies beyond France's borders. In peacetime, our mission is to carry out our work patiently, sensitively and with the utmost discretion. Our role is to strike decisively once a spy or double agent is identified. Now that war appears imminent ..."

He paused and shrugged expressively.

"We must become more proactive, but the necessity of absolute secrecy remains paramount. We are charged with identifying fifth columnists, the rats who infiltrate our cities in advance of the Nazi army, and discovering the battle plans, troop and weapon positions of the Nazi government. Your work will take you into enemy territory. I must emphasize the fragility of our position here. The discovery of our existence could have grave repercussions. Spies captured in peacetime usually end up before a firing squad. In war," he sighed. "capture is not an option. Torture is inevitable. Any betrayal will inevitably result in more deaths."

He reached into his jacket and produced a small glass capsule. "This is standard issue for all our operatives." The room fell into absolute silence as the colonel paused for a moment before continuing. "Cyanide. Quick and effective." He leaned back in his chair. "It's volunteers only. Are you still interested?"

Jacques stood up and saluted. "Yes, sir."

"Good man," the colonel said before continuing his briefing.

"We have ten men to protect the whole of France. It is not enough. In order to maximize our effectiveness, we are required to recruit 'honorable correspondents,' that is to say persons who are able to travel widely without attracting suspicion and who also have useful contacts. Persons who are willing, through use of their contacts and travel abilities, to obtain and pass to the bureau information which is potentially useful. Needless to say, these correspondents must be persons in whom we have the utmost confidence. They must be patriots prepared to risk their lives for France or alternatively persons demonstrably willing to sacrifice their own lives to prevent a Nazi victory. Care must be taken. It would be disastrous if we were infiltrated by double agents. There is another important criterion for these correspondents. They must provide their services for free." He shrugged. "We cannot afford to pay them.

Jacques, your official position here will be Captain, German Section, Counter-espionage, Responsibility Section, Paris. So, gentleman, to work."

Chapter 3

VESTINET, PARIS, 3 SEPTEMBER 1939

Josephine wrapped herself in her dressing gown and walked bare-foot down the staircase to the lounge. She glanced at the clock. It was nearly time. Impatiently, she twisted the knobs on the radio trying to locate the correct station through the crackling resistance. At last she could hear the distinctive sound of impeccable English accents.

The presenter announced Mr Chamberlain. It was 11.15 am as the British Prime Minister, in a somber voice, began his announcement.

"This morning, the British Ambassador in Berlin handed the German Government a final note stating that, unless we heard from them by eleven o'clock that they were prepared at once to withdraw their troops from Poland, a state of war would exist between us. I have to tell you now that no such undertaking has been received, and that consequently this country is at war with Germany."

She had been prepared for his words, but that did not lessen the shock she felt. She tried to stop the tears welling in her eyes as Chamberlain's precise tones continued as he explained the situation.

"We and France are today in fulfilment of our obligations going to the aid of Poland."

France too would join the war. Her heart stopped. There had

been no announcement from France. Not yet, but it seemed inevitable now. Britain was dragging France with her.

"Now may God bless you all. May He defend the right. It is the evil things that we shall be fighting against: brute force, bad faith, injustice, oppression and persecution. And against them I am certain that the right will prevail."

The broadcast ended. Josephine sat in silence staring at the radio, trying to process the implications of what she had heard. Slowly she stood up, distractedly trying to tune the

radio to a channel which could provide more detail regarding the situation in France. She noticed Paulette standing in open-mouthed silence at the door.

"Madam, what are we going to do?"

"It looks like we are going to fight," Josephine answered forcefully. "Pull yourself together; those Nazis won't beat us."

Josephine spoke firmly, but despite her show of fortitude, she shivered. Those hate-filled faces of the Brownshirt protesters in Berlin had never left her. They had invoked too many memories of that terror-filled night in St Louis to be either forgotten or dismissed as being of no consequence.

At noon France transmits its ultimatum to Germany to the effect that if it does not withdraw troops from Poland by 5.00 pm that day, France too will consider itself at war.

The evening paper carries a note from Georges Bonnet, French Ambassador in Berlin:

Following aggression against Poland by Germany, a state of war exists between France and Germany with effect from 3 September 1939 at 5 pm. The present notification is carried out in terms of Article 2 of the III Convention de La Haye of 18 October 1907, relative to opening of hostilities. Josephine threw the newspaper down. It was surreal. To send such a civilized note, in a manner following a strict protocol, to announce a state of war shocked her.

· · ·

War – the most obscene and uncivilized invention of man. The harbinger of tragic loss of human life and senseless destruction of property. If only this was not real. If only Pepito was still alive. If only she was in a café, surrounded by the Paris avant-garde. How they would have loved to dissect and hypothesize. If only ... if only.

Overcome with emotion, she brushed away tears. Hemingway, Fitzgerald, Dali, Picasso, Simenon, Joyce, Collette – how they would have discussed and debated, as they had done so many times. She could hear their voices whispering in her consciousness, impassioned and persuasive. Black and white. Right and wrong. Modernism, cubism, surrealism, creationism and Darwinism. War and peace.

Josephine shivered. She had never felt so alone. France, her beloved France, was at war with Germany, fighting to protect the country's fundamental principles of Liberty, Equality and Brotherhood, the very beliefs for which she had pledged herself to France. *Liberté, Egalité, Fraternité.* The beating heart of the French constitution, a constitution which had allowed her to flourish in her adopted country, while in the United States, the country of her birth, even as recently as that summer she had been excluded, humiliatingly, from hotels and vilified for her color.

The pleas for help uttered that terrible night in her hometown echoed through her memory. She recalled the reports of Kristallnacht, the night, the previous year, in Germany, when Jews had been murdered and their property ransacked. The Nazi regime was spreading like a deadly virus across Europe.

France must never become infected with that terrible sickness. The idea was repugnant. She pulled her dressing gown tighter around her. Chamberlain's words whirled round in her head.

She was not going to stand by. Nothing and no one would be allowed to steal away the liberties to which she had become accustomed in France. The bitter racism from which she had recently fled for the second time in her life must never be allowed to destroy her beloved Paris and France, not while she had breath in her body.

She picked up the telephone. She needed to know if her performance at the Casino de Paris would run that night as scheduled. The switchboard was jammed. She slammed down the phone.

"Paulette, call the driver. I'm going to the Casino. I can't stay here. I have to do something."

Chapter 4

DEUXIÈME BUREAU, PARIS, 17 SEPTEMBER 1939

Jacques leaned back in his chair as he glanced over the list of names Daniel Marouani had brought to him.

"I don't know." He shook his head as he tossed the paper onto his desk. He was satisfied that Daniel, his first recruit as an 'honorable correspondent,' could be trusted implicitly. Jacques had not needed much convincing that as a Jew, Daniel was fundamentally opposed to any future envisaged by the Third Reich. As one of the most successful theatrical agents in France, Daniel had many eminent contacts and was able to travel extensively without attracting attention. It was men like him that the bureau needed.

"It's too risky. She's not even French."

"I tell you," Daniel insisted. "She is more French than the French."

Jacques laughed. "She may well be, but she's show-business through and through. These people seem trustworthy and brave on the surface, but once they are put under pressure, they smash like glass."

"Not this one. She's as hard as nails."

"I'm sorry. It's my head on the block, yours too. I can't take the risk."

"Meet her, Jacques." Daniel implored, "I'm sure you won't regret it."

Jacques smiled. "You are serious, aren't you?" he said watching the intent expression on his friend's face. "We're talking about the same person? The scandalous Josephine Baker. The girl in the banana skirt. The topless dancer."

Jacques shook his head. "You know every 'honorable correspondent' has to have their background checked – thoroughly – before I can even approach them. It's common knowledge this woman thinks nothing of dancing naked in public and has an endless stream of lovers, both male and female. Hardly suitable material. I don't think we need to waste our time, do you? I cannot imagine she would be sanctioned. Even if she passed muster, there are too many parallels with Mati Hari. That is not a mistake we need to make twice." Jacques shook his head again. "An exotic promiscuous dancer turns spy. Come on, Daniel. You don't want to see her end up in front of a firing squad, do you?"

"Have you ever seen her dance?" Daniel sounded wistful. "She has the longest legs, the most marvelous body you could imagine."

"The length of her legs is not one of our criteria."

"Don't judge too quickly. She's black and married to a Jew, so there will be no place for her in Hitler's empire."

"She is American born and one of the most famous and richest women in the world. Why would she risk her life for France?"

"Meet her, Jacques. Where's the harm?"

"I'm going to take some convincing. An entertainer with her background ... it's too dangerous for us and for her. I don't want any of us to end up on the wrong end of a hangman's rope."

"I think she may convince you. She is very persuasive." Daniel winked. Jacques raised his eyebrows in surprise. "Why not start her with a low risk assignment and see how it pans out? Personally, I'm convinced of her suitability and would like to see her start as soon as possible. The woman has Europe in her pocket."

"She will be off back to America at the first whiff of danger." "She fled America to escape racial bigotry. I believe she will do everything she can to prevent the racism she abhors taking hold in her beloved France." Daniel crossed his arms over his chest and burst out singing, "J'ai Deux Amours."

Jacques laughed. "Very well. Make an appointment for me to see her, but I can't promise more than that."

Chapter 5

L'ASILE DES CLOCHARDS, PARIS, 1939

The Packard rolled slowly along the street. Josephine peered out of the rear passenger window searching for the address. "Stop, I can see it," she shouted. "Wait," she instructed as she climbed out, too impatient to allow her driver to descend and open the door for her. Josephine marched purposefully towards the Red Cross sign hanging above the dilapidated door. Some shabbily dressed children waved, and she paused for a moment to give them some sweets from her bag before smiling and pointing to the sign. "I have an appointment and mustn't be late," she explained. The children trailed after her full of curiosity. Josephine opened the door and walked inside closing it behind her.

An expensively dressed woman with dark, neatly rolled hair approached her. Her expression was one of disapproval and as she came closer, Josephine identified the woman's suit, which, while unmistakably Chanel, was of a design which had come out perhaps four years previously. The other ladies present in the hall turned towards Josephine, who ignored the general air of disapproval which seemed to meet her arrival.

They made her laugh, these women, with their serious faces and their constant preoccupation with their status. Was it any wonder that their husbands, the wealthy men of Paris, should look to younger more entertaining women to while away their leisure time? That they should search in the dancehalls and theatres of Paris for mistresses, for women like Josephine, who with their dancers' bodies and craving for adoration welcomed the attention.

Was it a suspicion that Josephine might have at one time or another seduced their partners that caused their unfriendly stares or maybe they were jealous of her clothes, the most stylish Paris could produce, or her fame or wealth or independence? Josephine didn't care. She hadn't come in search of friends.

"Where do I start?" she asked pulling off her gloves. One woman stepped forward. With a friendly smile and an outstretched hand. "Annette. Thank you so much for coming. I think we're going to need all the help we can get. I'll show you around." Annette chatted as she led Josephine from room to room.

"We're setting up beds here so that we can house more people. We're asking for donations of blankets and tinned food. We expect to have more and more refugees as the situation gets worse."

Josephine took the woman's arm. "Thank you. I needed to help."

The woman smiled. "Don't mind them," she said, nodding to the ladies who were still watching disapprovingly. "They'll thaw out eventually." Josephine tossed her hand and allowed her hips to sway provocatively.

"I won't mind them."

"I love listening to your records," Annette continued enthusiastically.

"Thank you." Josephine smiled.

"I hope the Casino de Paris reopens soon. Paris isn't the same with everything shut. I'd love to see you perform."

"We're rehearsing for a new show, 'London–Paris', everything has had to be changed because of the war. Opening night is the first of December. I'll give you tickets. I have rehearsals in the evenings, but I can come and help here in the afternoons. I will do whatever is needed. I have a pilot's license and I told them...," Josephine said, signaling with a nod to the watching group of ladies, "that I'm willing to fly supplies to wherever needed."

"That's wonderful," Annette said. "We do appreciate your volunteering. Let's just hope it's all over soon."

Chapter 6

VESINET

They peered through the impressive wrought-iron gates. A winding lane twisted its way through the mature oaks before arriving at the mansion house which peeped discreetly through the vegetation.

Jacques whistled under his breath. He wasn't even inside the grounds and the place exuded wealth and luxury like no private residence he had ever visited before. Maybe Daniel was right. It was worth the visit just to have a private audience with the infamous Josephine Baker. They rang the bell and waited for the gatekeeper to answer.

"Hello," a female voice called. Jacques couldn't see anyone at first, then a figure appeared from amongst the vegetation. Wearing denim dungarees and carrying a bucket, Mademoiselle Baker was not as he had expected.

She smiled, displaying the most beautiful set of white teeth he could imagine. Her eyes, immediately captivating, seemed to flirt with him, or maybe that was just his imagination or some base desire erupting from his primitive self. She casually fished about in her pockets, finally producing a large iron key with which she opened the gates. Daniel, an old acquaintance, she greeted with four alternate kisses on each cheek, but for Jacques, she held out her hand. Taking the proffered hand in his, he felt a shock of excitement as he touched her skin.

Daniel had warned him, but nothing could have properly prepared him. She seemed to exude sexual energy. He found his every expectation cartwheeling. He had expected a pampered celebrity; he had found Baudelaire's Black Venus.

"Mr Jack Fox." Daniel introduced him, using the undercover name Jacques had adopted for the meeting. Josephine leaned forward, taking his tie in her finger tips and pulling him towards her, so that they came closer and closer until their lips were almost touching. "I hope you don't mind if I call you Foxy," she whispered seductively.

She released the tie laughingly and then turned and said, "Come on, we can talk inside." She took Daniel's arm and swinging the bucket, explained she had been collecting snails. As they reached the entrance stairway, she put the bucket down on the steps and led them into the hallway. Jacques, or Jack as he had become, allowed his eyes travel around the entrance hallway. It was like entering a luxurious film set. A butler in white jacket and gloves appeared as if magically. He nodded discreetly towards Josephine. "Madame, if I had known."

"Don't worry, Bertrand." The voice – and the careless flick of the hand, both unique trademarks. "I was able to let our guests in. You may serve us in the library."

As they moved through the hallway with its marble stairs sweeping to the balcony and mezzanine above, Jack could not fail to be aware of the extraordinary wealth and privilege enjoyed by the occupant of this particular mansion. His heart sank, because, despite his reservations, from the moment of setting his eyes upon Josephine, he wanted to become part of her life, to recruit her as an 'honorable correspondent' if that was what she wanted. He'd do whatever it took.

But when he witnessed the surroundings which were her habitat, glanced into the dining room which could surely seat sixty people, he had to accept that someone who enjoyed such wealth, someone who could so easily buy their safety, would never assume the risks that accompanied the position of 'honorable correspondent.' This meeting would be his only opportunity to spend time with the charismatic Mademoiselle Baker.

They entered what was clearly the library. A fire was burning in the grate and armchairs were arranged around it. A chair, next to a writing desk stacked with letters were positioned to one side, and the remaining walls were lined floor to ceiling with books.

Again, Jack was conscious of the eyes of his hostess roving with approval over his body, or was he just imagining that. He caught her eye, and she winked mischievously. Jack would have blushed if he was not a man of the world. Handsome and athletic, he was accustomed to enthusiastic female attention.

Bertrand arrived with a tray, crystal champagne flutes and a magnum of Moët & Chandon in an ice bucket and uncorking the bottle with effortless skill, he filled their glasses. "Victoire," they toasted confidently.

"Close the door as you leave, Bertrand."

They sat down.

Jack began in formal fashion. "As you know, Daniel has recommended you as someone who could be of assistance to our war efforts. Our conversation is entirely confidential, you understand." Josephine, curled in her armchair, assumed a serious expression and nodded intently.

Jack leaned forward clasping his hands. He gestured with his eyes to the evidence of wealth around them.

"I'm sorry. It's too dangerous for you; for someone in your position. Why would you risk your life, your status, everything, for a fight that is not your own? You can cushion yourself from this war. It's not your fight. Go back to America, your home, while you still can."

Jack made as though to rise, but she was on her feet before he was, tears in her eyes and anger in her voice.

"How dare you!" "I came to this country with nothing. France welcomed me despite my color." She stretched out her wrists. "This color, for which I am despised in my native country. France made me. France gave me this." She gestured to her surroundings. "Without

France, I am nothing. I am ready to give my life to serve France. Use me as you will."

Jack felt ashamed. He had been so dismissive of her offer. The passion in her voice was clear. She meant every word she had said.

"Don't you understand?"

"I appreciate your sentiments." He tried to pacify her, yet he still could not let himself be swayed by the tantalizing Mademoiselle Baker. Reason had to prevail. "Although Daniel here has recommended that you be recruited as an 'honorable correspondent,' and you meet our criteria – there is no question of that – I understand that your application is born of patriotism and a desire to be of assistance, but we have to be realistic. It is simply too dangerous."

"I will not let the Nazis rob me of the freedom I found in this country. I am at your disposal."

"I can't let you do this unless I am convinced you understand just how dangerous the work can be." He glanced at Daniel. "We say 'honorable correspondent,' but an enemy might use the word 'spy'. Espionage is treason and the penalty, death. You have surrendered your American citizenship. I understand you intend to divorce, but at present you are married to a French citizen, a Jew. Your American birth cannot save you. You are French now and will be treated as such. Neither your fame nor your wealth will save you. Not if you are caught."

Josephine giggled mischievously and tapped him on the nose. "But, Foxy, I won't be caught."

"You must take this seriously," irritated by her flippancy.

"Why?" she asked, fluttering her eyelashes beguilingly. She flicked a hand. Then, in a more serious voice, "I am teasing you. Tell me what you want me to do."

"Be our eyes and ears. You are famous. You're invited to embassies around Europe. You mix with the elite of society. Listen. If you hear or see or discover anything, anything at all, which may be of interest, then let us know. But be careful, Josephine. Remember Mata Hari."

Josephine stood up, raised her hand in a salute as she slammed her feet together. "Baker, reporting for duty, sir."

"Congratulations," Jack and Daniel said in unison. "And welcome to the Deuxième Bureau," Jack added.

"Now let us celebrate my new career," and Josephine filled their glasses of champagne.

"To 'honorable correspondents.' Á Victoire."

It was dark by the time Jack and Daniel walked down the steps onto the grounds of the Baker mansion. A great deal of champagne had been consumed, in conviviality, in front of the roaring fire. The bucket still sat by the steps, but the snails had long gone. They would live to fight another day.

Chapter 7

THE FIRST ASSIGNMENT

It was with some trepidation that Jack drove through the gates of Le Beau Chêne, the name of Josephine's mansion in Vesinet. Since their last meeting, he had struggled to get the star out of his thoughts. She was like no other woman he had ever met. She had made her interest in him obvious at their first meeting – or was it just her enthusiasm to become an 'honorable correspondent'?

Maybe she liked to toy with men – all men. He could not pretend ignorance of her reputation as a seductress or even of his finding her attractive. He wondered if he would find himself in her sights, and if so, what his reaction would be.

Reason told him a liaison was impossible. Nothing and no one could be allowed to compromise the journey they were embarking upon. Yet the male within him could not fail to be excited at the prospect of an affair, however brief, with the intriguing La Baker.

As his car rolled to a stop before the steps, she opened the door wearing a lacy cream silk negligee and holding out a glass of champagne. "Jack, what kept you?" she scolded. "I am so excited. What have you found for me to do?"

His heart beat faster as he ran up the steps towards her. Just her presence made him feel good. She carried an air of mystery, of intrigue, infinitely more intoxicating than the glass of champagne in her hand. She kissed him on both cheeks. A light touch but sensuous. Jack felt the sexual energy between them as tangibly as an electric spark. She turned and led him into the lounge.

"We can talk privately here," she said closing the door. "Come sit beside me, here," she said patting the couch beside her. Jack could not avoid glimpses of her bare breasts and dusky nipples as the flimsy material of the negligee fluttered around her. Arousal tensed his whole body. Anxious to retain his authority and put some distance between them, he sat on the opposite chair and opened his brown leather briefcase to reveal two manila folders.

Josephine gave him a sulky look like a hurt child, then put on a serious face. "Yes, Jack," she said intently. "You have my full attention."

"We would like you to obtain an introduction to the Italian Ambassador in Paris. I have some background information and details of one of the employees there who might be careless with information. We need to find out what stand Mussolini intends to take so far as the outbreak of war is concerned. Do you think you can do that?"

Josephine smiled mischievously. "Of course." She stood up, strolled over to the telephone resplendent on a le Corbusier table, skimmed through the jewel-encrusted phone book beside it, and dialed.

She rattled instructions to the switchboard and seconds later in the most charming of voices she said, "Hello, it's Josephine Baker here. I would like to call on the Ambassador. Would tomorrow be suitable?" She made a note and put the telephone down.

"There," she said, winking. "It's done. I will report to you afterwards."

"Excellent. Well done. We shall have to be very discreet about our meetings. Telephone and letters are much too dangerous, and it is not safe for you to come to my office. I changed cars twice on the way here to make sure I wasn't followed."

"Of course," Josephine agreed. "Come for dinner tomorrow night. I can report to you then."

"Thank you," Jack agreed, immediately, excitement allied to anxiety.

"Well, it looks as if we are going to be seeing a lot more of each other," Josephine said, rising from her chair and moving towards him. She continued in a sultry voice. "Why, it's almost as if we're having an affair." She raised an eyebrow as she trailed a finger along Jack's shoulder. Jack felt a thrill of excitement. Being the attaché responsible for Josephine was going to be one hell of a brief.

Chapter 8

ITALIAN EMBASSY, PARIS

Josephine's car pulled up outside the Italian Embassy. She was a few minutes early and paused to check her makeup. She had dressed with particular care and was wearing an elegant drop waist shift in a demure style, reminiscent of the 1920s. She had selected her favorite fur, and with matching gloves, she was the epitome of sophistication. The guard waved her past without checking the proffered identification. As she arrived at the front door, it swung open, as if operated by an invisible attendant. She was ushered straight to the Ambassador's office and he welcomed her effusively. A middle-aged man with a generous belly, he seemed to swell with pride as he welcomed her.

"Mademoiselle Baker, we are most gratified that you have chosen to visit us."

Josephine nodded graciously. "I am delighted that you are able to welcome me at such short notice. After my recent visit to Italy, I was so impressed with the work of "Il Duce," I felt that I had to call. I had hoped you might be able to help me."

"Certainly." He gave a small bow. "It would be a pleasure to be of service."

"You see, I have a certain problem, but it's quite delicate."

"Please be assured of my utmost discretion."

"Yes, a very private matter. I am thinking of leaving Paris."

"Leave Paris? Mademoiselle Baker, Paris would not be the same without you."

"I had thought once that I would never be the same without Paris, but now with this war, nothing is the same. As you know, I am an American. I hope you do not find my transatlantic French accent too tiresome."

"On the contrary, you speak French most charmingly."

Josephine smiled. "Your Excellency is a diplomat. As I was explaining, I am an American. France is not my country. This is not my war." She leaned forward. "This is completely confidential, you understand."

"Don't worry, Mademoiselle." The diplomat placed a finger over his lips.

"I'm becoming frightened in Paris. I am alone in a very big house. I dread the Casino de Paris being forced to close permanently. And if I cannot dance, I will die. I was so charmed by your beautiful country. I am considering moving to Italy, permanently perhaps. Do you think I would be welcome?"

"Why certainly, Mademoiselle Baker. I myself would be delighted to show you the delights of my country."

"My only concern is that I do not want to escape from one war only to find myself in another. You understand."

"Of course, Mademoiselle. Your concern is only natural. I can assure you that Italy has no plans to enter the war. Indeed, I believe Italy is the haven you seek. I would be honored to provide every assistance should you decide to move. Rome is the most beautiful of cities, and for the summer, the Amalfi coast." He made a kissing gesture with his thumb and forefinger. "Magnifico."

"Thank you, your excellency. You have been most kind. Your Embassy is very beautiful. I think the most elegant I have visited."

"Let my attaché give you a tour of the public rooms. I think you will find the paintings quite exceptional."

"Your excellency is very kind." Josephine smiled brilliantly before turning to the military attaché who had been summoned.

"Here is the painting. The Embassy is very proud to have it here."

"It is very beautiful. I do like your uniform. You Italian men are so handsome."

"Thank you, Mademoiselle Baker," the man stuttered.

"How old are you? If you don't mind me asking."

"Thirty."

"There, we are practically the same age. We shouldn't be so formal," she whispered confidentially as she nudged him. "You are much too attractive for us to be on anything but the friendliest of terms," she said, fluttering her eyelashes again. She was pleased to see traces of a flush underneath her companion's tanned skin. "Now, what is your name?"

"Benito," he volunteered.

"Ah," she murmured. "Like your great leader. I had the pleasure of meeting him on my last tour. Such an inspirational man. Have you been in Paris long?"

"Only a few months. This is a new posting."

"And you are enjoying Paris, I hope?"

"I can't say that I know it well yet."

"I will leave you some tickets for my show. We will reopen in December. You will come, won't you?"

Josephine felt exactly like a cat stalking her prey. Once captured, there was the play. Tossing the victim into the air, letting it fall, letting it run, letting it think it could escape, before finally devouring it.

"Let me show you the library."

She tucked her arm around Benito's and hugged into his side, walking beside him with a familiarity most women would have reserved for a lover.

"What a somber room," she commented as she gazed around at the books which lined the walls. "I'm not a great reader myself," she confided.

"I think the Chinese Room may be more to your taste." Benito led her into the next room where cream walls were decorated with detailed murals of Chinese scenes.

"Yes, I love this," gushed Josephine fluttering her eyelashes. "What a beautiful building you work in."

As they strolled arm-in-arm into the next room, which, in keeping with the previous ones, boasted high ceilings and ornate chandeliers, Josephine was delighted to see an enormous globe in the middle of it. "Magnificent," she said, thrilled by the opportunity that she could see unravelling, if only she could keep her head.

Walking over to the globe, her heels clicking purposefully on the polished parquet, she touched the globe and whirled it with force. The earth revolved with satisfying speed.

"We call this the Map of the World Room," the soldier explained.

"I don't need to ask why," she joked. The globe dominated the otherwise unfurnished room.

"Let me show you the places I have travelled." The globe slowly glided to a halt and Josephine pointed to South America. "I recently returned from a tour there. I had planned to go back with a new show, but with this damned war ..." She shrugged. "I've had to change my plans. I am an American, you understand. All I care about is dancing. Politics ..." she said, as she flicked her hand in the air and sighed. "This war, it is so inconvenient. Curfew. Blackout. How is a girl supposed to live?" She rolled her eyes meaningfully. "I see you have seen active service," she commented, tapping one of the medals which lined Benito's chest. "Where have you been stationed? If it is not indiscreet to ask." She gazed into Benito's eyes.

He skimmed his hands over the globe. "Here, madam," he said, pointing to the tip of the boot that was Italy.

"And Northern Italy?" she asked, concentrating on remaining casual.

"I have been stationed here and here." He pointed to the positions as he explained.

"You must tell me all about it," Josephine murmured as they continued their tour.

As they wandered into the Sicilian Theatre, Josephine's eyes lit up. "This is more my style," giving Benito an exuberant wink. Approaching the far wall where a mural was framed, Josephine shed her ermine fur coat leaving it pooled on the polished floor, as irrelevantly as if it were discarded packaging.

The attaché followed, stooping to pick up the coat. His hands sunk into the fur and he could barely stop himself stroking the luxurious skin. How much had it cost? He could not even imagine. A clatter of heels grabbed his attention and he gulped as he saw Josephine erupt into a Charleston. He had heard about her performances, of course. After all, wasn't she the most famous woman in Paris? But to see her in person, so close. His eyes were glued to her form as she moved with boundless energy across the floor. Her eyes locked upon him, as if he was the only desirable man in the world. He felt his heart stop. Josephine Baker – *the* Josephine Baker – was dancing for him alone. Her legs moved and the skirt of her dress rose revealing her thighs. A shoulder strap slipped down her arm and he glimpsed her breast. She wasn't wearing a brassiere. He could feel a light glisten of sweat cover his skin. His mouth turned dry. His eyes were fixated on her. He had never felt like this before.

Suddenly, she stopped. He felt bereft, as if the dance should have lasted forever. Josephine walked towards him, laughing. "Dancing. That is all I care about. I shall dance until I die."

She placed a hand on his shoulder, looking intently at him with the dark soul of her eyes. Again, he could feel his heart beating. He was hers as surely as if their futures were bound together for eternity.

"Let's carry on," she said, tucking her arm in his and leading him forward. "I really appreciate your showing me around. I know how very busy you must be." She reminded him, again, that she would give him some tickets for her show. "You must promise to come." Benito nodded.

"Now tell me a bit about your work here. I imagine it is terribly important." Josephine could almost see her companion's chest swell with pride.

"I am responsible for signals. The French department is coordinated from the Embassy."

"Signals?" She waved her arms like semaphores. "What do you mean?"

"Messages, codes."

Josephine's eyes widened and she covered her mouth with her hand. "My goodness, how exciting."

She pulled the soldier more closely to her and whispered, "I don't suppose you could show me, could you?"

His face registered shock. Josephine chattered on. "I don't mean an actual message, you understand. Nothing secret. Of course, I wouldn't ask that, but I have heard that there are such things as coding machines. Imagine, if I could actually see one."

Benito glanced about. "Well, if you really want to. I suppose it wouldn't do any harm. You must promise not to tell anyone, though."

"Benito, it will be our secret."

Josephine studied the coding machine from behind a mask of feminine curiosity. It looked very much like a typewriter but was evidently much more complex. She listened intently as Benito laboriously explained its function. A thrill ran through her body. Espionage was exciting. She could feel the same high that she experienced with dance, with flying, with sex, with adventure.

Chapter 9

DEUXIÈME BUREAU, PARIS

Jack slammed the door of his office and cursed his damned bad luck. Weeks of work were lost because Monsieur Deloitte had chosen that particular moment on that particular day to wear a blue coat and stroll along the Boulevard de La Madeleine.

The operation had run like clockwork. Almost a month previously, they had, through phone tapping surveillance on the German Embassy in Paris, intercepted a telephone call between a person calling himself Georgette, and a secretary on the diplomatic staff at the Embassy. The person had been providing information about French troop movements and mobilization in Paris. A spy operating in the city. He had to be caught and soon. They had managed to set up a telephone call diversion system which allowed them intercept calls to the German Ambassador. Once in place, all they had to do was listen and wait for the spy to call again. It had taken days of patience until the finally, that morning, the voice of Georgette had come on the line.

Jack had signaled for the call to be interrupted. "The ambassador's secretary here," he answered. "He is engaged at present but has instructed me to meet you to clarify the information you provided earlier."

"I will come immediately," Georgette replied.

"No, not to the Embassy. It is too dangerous. Where are you? Let me meet you at outside the main entrance of La Madelaine. I will have a Lincoln car with diplomatic number plates and a driver in uniform. I will sit in the back. If you climb inside the car, we can talk privately."

"You will recognize me?"

"Of course."

"In any case, it will be easy for you to see me. I am wearing a blue raincoat and a beret. I will be with my wife, who will be carrying a grey umbrella."

"Excellent."

Jack put down the phone. "We're on," he said, grabbing his coat as he ran from the office. The two policemen who had been assigned to assist him with the mission were waiting in a nearby café with the disguised car parked outside. At his signal, they gulped down their café noirs and joined him. Soon they were driving through the heavy rain to the rendezvous. Because of the weather, there were very few pedestrians. Jack waited. And waited. Six pm came and went, then five-past, then ten-past. He glanced at his watch in irritation. Had Georgette realized he was being lured into a trap? At quarter past six, a man in a blue raincoat approached. He stopped at the car and studied the front and then walked slowly alongside peering in the window. Jack smiled at the man. He was alone, but it must be Georgette. It had to be. Jack swiftly climbed out of the car and signaled to the man to get in.

"Come on," Jack instructed, taking the stranger's arm. "We can talk privately in the car."

The other pulled free and made to run. Jack grabbed him and they both fell to the pavement. The police officers climbed out of the car, handcuffed the man who was protesting vociferously and bundled him into the car. They took him to the police headquarters for processing and to be interviewed. After intensive questioning it was apparent that the man they had captured was not Georgette but an innocent passer-by who had by coincidence triggered their trap. Jack hoped Josephine had better news.

Chapter 10

VESINET, PARIS

Josephine leaned back in the armchair, taking a sip from the flute of champagne which Jack handed to her. Her eyes sparkled and danced as she tossed the code book towards him.

"I told you," she teased.

Jack snatched the book from the air and leafed through the pages. Incredibly, it appeared to be exactly what she claimed – sets of codes for the commercial Enigma machine which the Deuxième Bureau suspected the Italians used to send confidential messages. If it was genuine, and it appeared to be, its procurement was the feat of an accomplished agent, something well beyond the remit of an 'honorable correspondent.'

"How on earth...?"

She chuckled and tossed her head before tilting it sideways and looking at him.

"Didn't you notice?" She took the book back and flipped it open. "He even signed it!"

Jack shook his head. "The signature alone is enough to get him shot."

"It's last month's, that's why he said he could give it to me. It was going to be thrown out."

"This is fantastic, Josephine. This, together with all the information you have about troops and ports and the Italians' intentions, generally, will be invaluable."

Josephine twisted and pulled up her skirt revealing her thigh, so he could see the ink scribbled notes which covered her skin. "I made an excuse of needing the toilet so I could write reminders."

She leaned forward. "Toast," she exclaimed. "To my first mission. A success. My new career – as a spy!"

They clinked glasses looking intently into each other's eyes – as is customary in France.

Jack held her gaze. It was difficult not to. She was, without doubt, the most intriguing woman he had ever met or could ever hope to meet. He felt her eyes, not for the first time, rove over his body, making him very conscious of his single state. It would not do to be married around Mademoiselle Baker, that was certain. Still, he could not get involved. No matter how much he was physically drawn to her. No matter how willing she appeared to be. She was much too dangerous. Again, the shadow of Mata Hari swept over him. The parallels were there, too obvious to be ignored. A woman, a beautiful woman, recruited by the French as a spy. A woman who fell in love with a German she was supposed to be spying on. Or maybe she had just been doing what she had been asked to do. The evidence had been inconclusive, but the result had been final. Mata Hari had been condemned as a traitor and shot by a French firing squad. He had recruited Josephine. She was his responsibility now. If anything happened to her, the fault would be his and his alone.

Interrupting his thoughts, she approached him. Hips swaying. Her lips parted in a sultry smile. There was no mistaking her intentions. She reached out to caress his cheek. He grabbed her wrist and gripped it tightly.

"This isn't a game."

"Isn't it?" She hissed as she struggled to break free.

"You don't understand the risks."

"Do I look like a child?"

"You could get shot."

She laughed as if he was an idiot.

"I won't put your life at risk."

She repeated, "Do I look like a child?" Then went on, "Don't you think I have the right to make my own decisions?" Her eyes flared.

God, he thought, she was attractive. He shook her wrist.

"If you want this, you need to promise something." Now he had her attention. "Me, only me."

She laughed.

He released his hold on her wrist and stepped back from her.

"That is my condition. Women talk when they are in bed. If you want it, me, only me, until this is finished."

She glared at him, eyes flashing angrily, like she wasn't used to being refused.

He turned to go. He was done.

"Wait, Jack." Her voice was low and sexy, caressing his body, as sensuous as fine silk. He turned. He knew he shouldn't, but like Medusa, her eyes compelled. Her whole demeanor had changed. Now she was a seductress. And so he understood how she was able to obtain information so effortlessly. She was redoubtable. But he was Jacques Abtey, albeit masquerading as Jack Fox. He was a soldier of the French Army. He had sworn allegiance to France. He was a Captain in the Deuxième Bureau charged with the protection of Paris. He could say no. And the words were there on his lips. But she glided silently towards him and placed a finger over his mouth. Silencing him. Still, he refused to succumb.

He made a sharp move away from her.

"No," he said louder than he had intended. "It is too dangerous, for you," he added immediately, in case she thought he could not control himself.

"But what if I agree?" she asked. And her eyes widened as she stared into his. "J'ai d'accord. Only you. For as long as it lasts."

He could feel the champagne glass in his hand and soon they were toasting an alliance like no other. Jack was so infused with desire he pushed the shadows from his thoughts. They were at war. Everything was different.

Chapter 11

MAGINOT LINE, NOVEMBER 1939

"Encore! Encore!" Shouts and whistles rose above the thunderous clapping as Josephine curtsied and made yet another attempt to finish her set. The manager signaled her towards him and finally despite the audience's pleas, she left the stage.

She glanced back from the wings, the faces of the young soldiers were jubilant in expectation for her return as their feet stamped determinedly on the floor. She glanced at the stage manager. It was his decision. He tilted his head subtly in the direction of Maurice Chevalier who was approaching with an angry stride, then shook his head. Josephine began to walk towards her dressing room. Chevalier hissed "you'll be old one day" under his breath as he passed her and strode onto the stage. Josephine smiled as the cries for her return stopped on his appearance and a silence indicative of disappointment fell over the makeshift theatre.

General Chevrolet appeared just as she reached her designated dressing room.

"Josephine, you were amazing. We are so grateful. Performances like this make a huge difference to the soldiers' morale. They know they are not forgotten."

"I'm sorry I went over schedule. It was difficult to leave when there were so many encores. I'm afraid I have upset Maurice."

The General chuckled. "Don't worry, my dear. It's no surprise to me that they prefer to watch you rather than him. We have had to be strict about times because the soldiers have a curfew." He glanced at his watch. "The show will have to wind up at ten exactly."

"Maurice is going to have a very short set."

The General laughed. "Well, he insisted on taking the second half of the performance. I would like to take you on a tour, if you don't mind, "he went on. "Just a small thank-you for coming to see us. We are very proud of our underground fortresses. They are impenetrable from air and artillery attack. He led Josephine to a railway platform. A train appeared and as the General signaled, they boarded. "The trains link the fortresses and defensive outposts. We have everything we need here to survive a siege," he continued proudly. "Our troops are specially trained and are an elite division of the French army."

Josephine made suitable gasps of approval when the General paused for breath and was relieved she did not have to take notes. The visit to the fortress was so charged with compromising military information, she would have struck gold had she been a double agent. Yet as they toured the underground fortress, she experienced a dark foreboding.

During the frantic rehearsals for the London–Paris show and her whirlwind and unexpected romance with Jack, it had been easy to be lulled into a false sense of security as the press dubbed the declarations of war by Britain and France and the ensuing weeks as the "Phony War," yet here in the buried stronghold constructed specifically to fend off the Nazi threat, Josephine felt increasingly uneasy.

The General explained enthusiastically the fortifications of the Maginot Line as they wandered from the generator room, through the kitchen and operating theatre to the dormitories, and in the warren of underground streets in an underground city where day and night were replaced with the glare of electric lights and where there was no gentle breeze to disrupt the heavy, oppressive air. Instead of being reassured by the General's confidence in the defenses under his command, she felt bile rising in her stomach and a terrible sense of foreboding.

Chapter 12

VESINET, CHRISTMAS EVE 1939

Bertrand pointed towards the library. Jack whistled cheerfully as he opened the door. He had managed to finish early and hoped to enjoy an intimate hour or so with Josephine before she left for the Casino. She barely looked up. "I have to get this finished before I leave."

He shook his head. "But what are you doing?" She was kneeling on the floor in front of the fire surrounded by toys of every description.

"Wrapping," she answered with some irritation. "And I need your help?"

He sat down beside her and picked up a toy car and began to cut some paper. "Not that," she scolded. "That." She nodded to a red suit draped over the armchair.

"Oh, no," he groaned. "I only have a few hours' leave. It's Christmas," he added hopefully, as he winked at Josephine.

"Not yet," she answered sharply. "You need to put that on. If we go now, I will have time to give these out before the show." She nodded to several sacks of presents which were positioned beside the doorway. Knowing there was no escape, Jack donned the Father Christmas suit and with a jolly "Ho! Ho! Ho!" he swung the bags of gifts over his shoulder. Josephine smiled with delight and they drove off. They arrived at Maubeuge, one of Paris's less salubrious districts. Her arrival was expected, and a long queue of children were already waiting patiently. Josephine looked particularly stunning, having worn one of her most glamourous evening dresses for the occasion. Jack thought with amusement that it was not often that Father Christmas was upstaged as the

children swarmed around his companion. The time flew by and soon the sacks were empty. The grateful smiles from the children made it all worthwhile, and not for the first time, Jack found his heart breaking. As Josephine distributed the presents, the happiness which shone from her face as a result of the pleasure she was giving was heart-warming. He found himself wondering, for all her poise and elegance, just how far she had really travelled from that scrawny kid in St Louis who longed every Christmas for a present, just like those she could now distribute so effortlessly. When she managed to tear herself away from the children, promising to return with more gifts soon, they climbed into the car and the vehicle roared to life as Josephine slammed her foot down on the accelerator.

"We're not in a race – or are we?" Jack asked, checking over his shoulder.

"Did you see the girls wearing red coats?"

Jack barely had time to nod.

"They are the daughters of the manager of the department store where I ordered the gifts. He knew I was distributing presents and must have arranged for them and their friends to be taken here."

Jack shrugged.

"Don't you see? I want children who wouldn't otherwise have a present at Christmas to have a gift to open. Those kids from wealthy families don't need me. I won't tell anyone next time I'm going to do this. Except you, Jack." She leaned across and kissed his cheek. "You, chéri, are indispensable."

Chapter 13

PARIS, 10 MAY 1940

The woman ruffled in her skirt pocket before finally presenting a green jewel. "Emerald. It's real, I promise."

Her face was exhausted and grey, with eyes that had not slept for days. She carried one child on her back and there were another two beside her, all with dark hair and large eyes. Josephine glanced at her watch. Her audience could wait, their bellies and purses were full, but these people needed her help. She reached out, closing the woman's fingers around the precious stone. "You don't need that here. Keep it safe." She glanced at the children. "Here," she said, holding out a small piece of chocolate to each one. Their faces lit up as though she was giving them gold. The woman smiled, but it did not reach the weariness in her eyes.

"You can stay here," Josephine said. "I'll find you a place." She strode along the rows of humanity lining the hall. "Here," she said, beckoning. "You can sleep here."

The woman grasped her hand. "Thank you, Madame."

Josephine stood beside them as they set down their baggage. It wasn't much. A small suitcase. A brown paper parcel tied with string. All that remained of their life before. She found some more sweets amongst her pockets and gave them to the children.

Annette arrived, pointing at the clock. "Go, Josephine. I'll take over."

Josephine waved goodbye. Annette whispered to the refugees, "That was Josephine Baker, you know. She is a volunteer here. She has a performance tonight at the Casino de Paris, so she can't wait."

"I didn't recognize her," said the woman.

Annette laughed. "No. She wears a uniform here, like the rest of us. But tonight, she will be the most glamorous woman in Paris."

Josephine ran past the doorman, shedding clothes with every step. Daniel was tapping his watch. She signaled a thumbs-up followed by a three. Jack was waiting for her in her dressing room. "Any news?" he asked.

"Nothing suspicious," she answered, and with a graceful movement, flung her panties onto the chair and grabbed her costume. "Help me in," she instructed, turning her back. Jack deftly did up the catches.

"Keep watchful. The spies, the fifth columnists, arrive with the refugees. They are the scum that form the army vanguard."

Josephine nodded and then kissed him lightly on the mouth. "I got it, and what's more," she added teasingly. "I've got that invite you wanted." Jack's eyes widened. She giggled. "Yes. Saturday, I am going to the Japanese Embassy. Is there anything particular you want to know?"

"Just keep on doing what you do." Jack laughed and Josephine wiggled her hips provocatively.

"I sure am."

"Break a leg," Jack called after her as she ran from the dressing room.

Chapter 14

PARIS, 16 MAY 1940

Jack slammed down the telephone. "Come at once," she had said. Fear gripped his heart as he ran down the stairs. She had never telephoned the bureau before. She knew how dangerous it was. Something must be seriously wrong. The journey to the Red Cross refuge dragged as Jack in turmoil wondered what had caused Josephine's urgent call. His anxiety forced him to face just how much Josephine had come to mean to him. While life with her was impossible, life without her was unimaginable.

He stared morosely out of the car window. Paris was no longer gay. As she swelled with refugees fleeting before Hitler's army, a more somber persona had evolved. Police combed the streets, passing from one person to another checking identity papers, searching for the dreaded fifth columnists, who according to press reports, lurked at every street corner. Suspicion and fear hung around the city, imposing a damp greyness as dank and impenetrable as the worst spring fogs. The cars which now clogged the streets had mattresses tied to the roofs and cooking paraphernalia draped from the luggage racks. Their drivers had come to Paris seeking safety, not frivolity.

When he arrived at the refuge, there was no sign of Josephine.

Anxiously, he started towards the door. Annette approached him. "There, Jack," she said pointing. Then he saw her, on her knees before an elderly man, soothing his swollen and blistered feet with a poultice. "Josephine," he shouted relieved to see her. She turned and smiled gently indicating he should wait. Her patient was seen to relax under her ministrations and Jack found himself acknowledging that it was no wonder he had become

captivated by Josephine. She had that effect on everyone around her. Even the snobbish elite amongst the Red Cross volunteers had warmed to her eventually. Once her patient's foot was soundly bandaged, Josephine joined him. Taking Jack's arm, she whispered in his ear. "I want you to check out some men who arrived today. They're in their twenties. Aryan in appearance. I'm sure they are fifth columnists." Jack could see the men, standing and chatting casually together. They were certainly Germanic in appearance.

"You are marvelous," he said, resisting the urge to kiss her on the cheek. "I'll check them out. Meantime," he turned her towards him and looked her directly in the eye. "You have done what I said?"

She nodded, and then giggled mischievously. "I've been filling the empty champagne bottles with petrol. I've enough to get to Milandes."

"Promise me you are telling the truth."

"Yes, Jack. I have sent the best furnishings already."

"You must leave the moment I send word. You understand." He leaned forward whispering again. "The government are already burning confidential papers. We expect to evacuate soon if there is no improvement. I might not be able to come personally. This might be the last time we see each other. Whatever happens, I must know that you are safe at Milandes."

Josephine leaned forward, brushing a finger sensually along his jaw as she did so. "Do not worry, Jack, we will meet again."

She turned then in answer to a call for help from Annette. Jack watched her disappear into the melee of humanity which now packed the center. Then he focused on the suspects. If his suspicions were correct, they were deserters from the German army. Men with no taste for brutality and murder, but he had not wanted to tell Josephine that. He did not want to discourage his most enthusiastic 'honorable correspondent'.

Chapter 15
18TH JUNE 1940

Abbreviated translation of speech by General de Gaulle

The French government, after having asked for an armistice, now knows the conditions dictated by the enemy.

The result of these conditions is the complete demobilisation of the French land, sea and air forces, the surrender of our weapons and the total occupation of French territory. The French government would come under German and Italian tutelage.

It can be said that this armistice is not only a capitulation, but that it reduces our country to slavery. A great many Frenchmen refuse to accept either capitulation or slavery, for reasons which are called: honour, common sense and the higher interests of the country...

...The Polish, Norwegian, Belgian, Netherlands and Luxemburg governments, though driven from their territories, have thus interpreted their duty. ...

...I say the higher interests of the country, for this is not a Franco-German war to be decided by a single battle. This is a world war. No one can foresee whether the neutral countries of today will not be at war tomorrow, or whether Germany's allies will always remain her allies. If the powers of freedom ultimately triumph over those of servitude, what will be the fate of a France which has submitted to the enemy?

Honor, common sense, and the interests of the country require that all free Frenchmen, wherever they be, should continue the fight as best they may.

It is therefore necessary to group the largest possible French force wherever this can be done. Everything which can be collected by way of French military elements and potentialities for armaments production must be organized wherever such elements exist.

I, General de Gaulle, am undertaking this national task here in England.

I call upon all French servicemen of the land, sea and air forces; I call upon French engineers and skilled armaments workers who are on British soil, or have the means of getting here, to come and join me.

I call upon the leaders, together with all soldiers, sailors and airmen of the French land, sea and air forces, wherever they may now be, to get in touch with me.

I call upon all Frenchmen who want to remain free to listen to my voice and follow me.

Long live free France in honor and independence!

Chapter 16

MILANDES, 23 JUNE

Her hands began to tremble as she stared in horror at the front page of the newspaper. Tears began to form, blurring the printed words, however, the photograph became more vivid. Imprinted in her mind as forcibly as if she were there and witnessing it with her very own eyes. A sign at the train station in Montpon–Menesterol indicating Negros were not welcome in the Occupied Zone. Josephine sank down into her arm chair. All thoughts of eating the breakfast of scrambled egg with toasted bread, which Paulette had prepared, gone. Her coffee grew cold as she tried to quantify the implications of the article. Her body grew cold and she began to shiver. The feelings of safety which had surrounded her the moment she arrived at her chateau and refuge dissipated. Montpon was only one hundred kilometers away.

An ordinary market town close to the departmental border between Dordogne and Gironde. An arbitrary point on a map where the Nazi forces had chosen to place a border control point. The location could just have easily been Sarlat. By the stroke of a General's pen she might even by now have been expelled from her home and on her way to a holding-camp for those the Germans and their French followers regarded as unwanted and disposable. Memories swamped her. How far and how fast must she run to escape? Could she once again learn to live under a cloud of fear and uncertainty? Now it would be different. She had sampled freedom. When she had been a child, she had known none. Infused amongst her first memories was a sense of fear. A knowledge ingrained from birth that she was different. Black. Segregated. Always lurking in her childhood there had been a terror of the Ku Klux Klan and all that they stood for and represented. Horrific lynchings and beatings had terrorized the communities of her childhood. Ultimately, she had fled America to escape, and now ... the armistice France had entered into with Germany had divided France into two. One part directly ruled by Germany, the other part, in which she now found herself, by a government in Vichy. One that she knew shared many of the political and social views held by the Germans. Because of her color, she could no longer return to Paris. Because she had renounced her American citizenship and become French she no longer enjoyed the same rights of travel. Because she had assumed the Jewish religion of her spouse, her very safety was now at risk. *Well,* she told herself, as she ripped the front page of the newspaper to sheds, *we'll see about that!*

Chapter 17

MILANDES, JULY 1940

Jack threw down the map. Ahead, the road that he had been following had narrowed into little more than a footpath, obviously impassable for a car. Both sides of the road were flanked with ditches making it impossible to turn.

He twisted round to navigate as he reversed, and it was then he saw the turrets winking at him through the oak trees that lined the fields.

That had to be it. Just as Josephine had described. A fairy tale castle perched on the hillside. Les Milandes was clearly one of the medieval chateaux constructed to defend the Dordogne Valley from invaders. He could not help but wonder how she would fare under the current invasion. He pressed hard on the accelerator and the car sped back down the narrow twisting road while the roar of the engine rattled through the tranquil rural scenery, as out of place as the tanks in Paris.

After a few more dead ends, he finally rolled to a stop outside the chateau. Jack stepped out of the car, taking a moment to admire the building, which with its turrets and ramparts could easily have been transported directly from a story book. He hoped Josephine had made it safely. He had not stopped worrying about her since he had telephoned her to tell her the army was evacuating Paris and to leave immediately. The weathered oak door of the chateau began to swing open. He could just discern the outline of a figure peering out from the shadowed hallway. Then a shrill shriek, "Foxy!" and she was in his arms. How good it felt to have her back where she belonged. Their mouths met. How long had it been? Forever.

They stood, clasped in each other's arms, then gently Jack began to untangle himself. He stood Josephine in front of him. Holding her arms, he looked directly into her eyes and said, "I have some terrible news." Her eyes clouded as she stared at him blankly. There had been a lot of terrible news in the last few weeks. "Captain Jacques Abtey has died." He bowed and twirled out his hand in a theatrical gesture. "Let me introduce myself, I am Jack Saunders, American, of course, your ballet instructor."

Josephine began to smile. Taking his hand, she continued the pantomime. "Delighted to meet you."

"Yes, I am Jack Saunders, Jacques Abtey's – Foxy's – closest friend. It was his dying wish that I should come and visit you in order to relay the sad news. I have been appointed as the Captain's executor, and I will be dealing with his affairs from now on. It was terribly sad," he continued in a somber voice. "A young man stolen from us in the flower of his youth, on the seventeenth of June, immediately after Pétain's announcement that France would seek an armistice with Germany. Robbed of his life just as peace was about to be declared. Such a handsome, virile young man!"

Josephine shrieked with laughter. It was good to see her in such high spirits. She grabbed his arm and tucked in beside him as she led him towards the doorway.

As they walked into the chateau, Jack asked casually, "Have you by any chance heard of General Charles de Gaulle?"

She shook her head, her expression serious. "Do you forget I am an artiste? I have never been called for military service. Why would I have heard of him?" She winked and reached up and whispered in his ear, "Foxy, when are we going to London?"

Later, much later, when they were ensconced in front of the fireplace sipping champagne, it was time to talk properly.

"What happened, Josephine?"

As soon as I got your call, I loaded up the car, myself, Paulette and the Belgian couple I met at the shelter. And I took the animals, of course, and drove like crazy to get here. We were lucky. We arrived here on the seventh of June. Your phone call saved us. Thank you."

"It was the least I could do." Jack raised his glass. "There has to be some perks with being an 'honorable correspondent'."

"What about you? I've been so worried."

"We gathered up the files, all the compromising information that we didn't want to burn. We couldn't leave the Nazis the names and addresses of all our 'honorable correspondents', could we? Once the lorries were loaded, we headed for Tours. The roads were clogged with refugees. It was a terrible journey. Finally, we arrived at the Camp de La Courtine, it was there that I heard the name of Charles de Gaulle for the first time. Soldiers were gathering there from all over France, but it was chaos. Some wanted to fight on, some argued we were bound by the armistice. Trying to organize some kind of defense seemed impossible. The generals could not agree. The government was in chaos. But those who wanted to fight were talking about de Gaulle and getting to London.

I was sent on to the Abbey of Bon-Encontré near Agen. The monks made up a dormitory for us. Twenty beds with mattresses and blankets. I was supposed to stay there, but I couldn't get what I had heard about de Gaulle out of my head. I left the abbey four days later with some like-minded friends. I've made contact with Paillole. He asked me to join him. He intends to reorganize the counter-espionage unit to work clandestinely in Vichy until the Nazis are defeated. But after what I heard about de Gaulle, I've decided to go to Britain, Josephine, and join the Free French Forces. It's risky, though. The sinking of the French ships at Mers-el-Kébir by the Royal Navy has caused a great deal of bad feeling. It's not inconceivable that Vichy France could declare war on Britain and then where will we be?"

Josephine nodded sadly. "Nearly one thousand three hundred sailors lost. Who would have believed it would come to this?"

"Still it shows the British mean to fight on. They couldn't risk the French fleet being incorporated into the Nazi forces. There'll be a warrant for my arrest issued by now. I am a deserter. I refuse to accept this armistice. I must get to London."

"Me too," Josephine said enthusiastically. "I will come with you. I've been listening to de Gaulle on the radio. Every day."

"I will contact Paillole about you. As a deserter from the French Forces and a male under forty, there is no way I can leave France legitimately. But I have to do something. I don't trust the Nazis or this Vichy Government. I believe in de Gaulle."

"I agree." Josephine stood up and raised her glass. "To London and the Free French Forces." They toasted.

Josephine laughed as she showed Jack the radio transmitter hidden behind the paneling in the tower. "Did you seriously think I would stay here and do nothing? Here is perfect for broadcasting. It's one of the highest points in the area."

Jack shook his head. "You do realize how dangerous it would be if a transmission is traced to here."

She winked. "Don't worry. There are no vehicles in the area capable of tracing the signal. That is information that I'm careful to obtain. Anyway, it's not being used. Not yet.

We are getting ready for the resistance. We are so close to the border with Occupied France that this area is bound to be important. And it won't be too difficult to get information from the Forbidden Zone. We are not so far from Bordeaux and the coast here."

Jack gazed from the tower window down the Valley of the Dordogne. A view that had not changed for centuries. He could almost see the gabares, moving down the river with their distinctive sails billowing in the breeze, which hundreds of years ago would have carried their precious wine cargo to Bordeaux, then a global port for distribution around the world. Perched along the cliff tops that towered either side of the valley above the River Dordogne, the fortifications blended into the rocks of which they were part as they had done for centuries. She was right. This isolated corner of Dordogne, with its narrow twisting lanes was impassable for many military vehicles. Steep cliffs and heavy forestation could offer perfect terrain for a resistance movement. The Valley of the Dordogne had withheld the English in the Hundred Years War and now he hoped she was ready to withstand a new enemy.

Josephine took his hand, pulling him away. "I have some more things to show you, then you can meet the others."

Jack shook his head in astonishment as he studied the shotgun. "Where did you get these?" he asked as she waved to the assortment of guns cleverly hidden behind one of the massive wine kegs in the cellar.

Josephine shrugged. "You can't expect me to tell you all my secrets." She tapped his nose. "It's for your own safety."

Jack caught her and pulled her to him. "Tell me," he growled, "or I won't let you go." Josephine twisted into his body, lightly planting a kiss on his lips.

"I might like that." Then she giggled flirtatiously and flicked her eyelashes. "Actually, I want to tell you. The villagers didn't want to hand in their guns. They need them for hunting. The blacksmith made this opening behind the barrel and then sealed it closed. No one would find it unless they knew it was here. We have to get ready."

This time, Jack was angry. "Josephine, how many people know?"

She shrugged.

"How many?"

"Just me and the blacksmith."

Jack sighed with relief. At least it wasn't the whole village, he thought.

"And the rest of the team." Josephine added with a radiant smile. "Come on, it is time for you to meet them."

Chapter 18

MILANDES, BASTILLE DAY 1940

The July sun moved across the sky unnoticed as midday slipped to late afternoon. A cool breeze rustled through the leaves of the oak trees creating a gentle backdrop to the chatter from the gathered guests. The sky was cloudless, a deep azure blue.

The celebration was a culmination of preparations which had been going on for days. There were easily forty people seated upon the benches that lined either side of the long trestle tables positioned strategically on the terrace to take advantage of both the shade from the trees and the panoramic views.

Josephine had laughed when Jack had carried one of the red velvet armchairs from the dining room and placed it at the head of the table, insisting she sit there, but she had taken her place and curtsied as everyone clapped.

The meal had begun with an aperitif. Jean Claude had produced some eau de vie d'abricot for which it seemed his wife was famed. The recipe was apparently a closely guarded secret, but after a sip of the rich cordial, it didn't surprise Josephine to learn that the estimated alcohol content was high. The table was replete with baskets of rustic bread, freshly baked, plates of foie gras, the pâté for which the Dordogne was famous, charcuterie and olives. Wine was poured and the feast began in earnest.

The aroma of roasting wild boar and smoke drifted across her nostrils, as the direction of the wind changed. She glanced across at Phillipe, who had insisted on taking charge of cooking the boar which had been culled for the feast. Watching it turn on the spit, she was conscious how little the twentieth century had touched Milandes.

The scene, which was playing before her, had changed little since the chateau had been built in 1489 at the behest of the Chatelaine of Castelnaud. When Lord Caumont, Lord of Castelnaud, had gathered his subjects together to celebrate the great feasts of their day, the menu surely was much the same. The drinks identical. The pleasure of people gathering together to enjoy good conversation and excellent food. If they could manage to laugh a little under the shadow of the war which engulfed the whole of Europe, surely the previous occupants had managed to put their difficulties aside on days as beautiful as this one. She struggled for a moment trying to remember what might have troubled the great lord then shook her thoughts away. She wanted to enjoy the day. One day they had stolen from Hitler. When the war was over, she would be able to immerse herself in the history of her home and the lives of its previous occupants. Her eyes wandered to Jack. Jean Leon had exited stage left so very recently to make room for his replacement at stage right. Jean had come visiting perhaps hoping for a reconciliation, but while she had found herself unable to refuse him and his family refuge until the false papers they as Jews would require to leave France could be obtained, she had no wish for him to return to her bed. "Foxy", as she still liked to call Jack in their most private moments, had taken a firm hold of her heart and for the moment she had no wish to interfere with her current very satisfactory arrangements. Jack was a thousand miles and a lifetime apart from any of her past lovers. Direct and as succinct with words as actions, she had found herself aroused by his refusal to be impressed by either her fame or her wealth. His fitness, appropriate for a military man, and his body in terms of firmness and muscle matched those of her most able dancers. He was slow to anger, which was a relief given her tempestuous nature. In her experience, his decisiveness and direction was unparalleled, but his most intoxicating quality was his commanding presence. To date, she had found herself bound by his command virtually without question. And coupled with a natural yet tangible aura of security which seemed to hang around him, meant in the dangerous times in which they now found themselves, she would require some considerable persuasion to part with her "Foxy" no matter how tempting an offer she received. She smiled to herself as she remembered the trace of his touch over her body. Phillippe approached the table to announce that the pig was ready and laid generous plates of sliced meat at strategic points along the table. The diners cleaned their plates with chunks of bread, then filled them again, spiking the juicy meat with forks. Madame Lebras carried to the table the hot potatoes they had cooked earlier. Then came the salads. Madame Dumas had brought fresh tomatoes from her garden, sliced finely and served with onions and lettuce. Madame Bouscat produced her lemon cordial as an aperitif to clean the palate between the main course and the dessert. It was a reflection of the significance of the gathering as this was a treat usually reserved for weddings and Christmas. The heavy sweet liqueur was delicious, and with an unquantifiable alcohol content, the portions were suitably modest. Dessert followed. As if magically, the tables filled with tartes tatin, which the women of the village had prepared and had kept cool under linen napkins tucked away in wicker baskets beneath the tables. Josephine never failed to be impressed by these offerings. Not so much for the taste, although they were invariably delicious, especially if served with cream kept cool in the stone presses that served as fridges in the remote farmhouses, but by the attention to detail of the bakers who had made them. Whether the tartes were comprised of apples, pears, apricots or one of the rarer fruits which seemed to grow with such abundance in the area, there was an extraordinary skill required to make each segment identical in size as if measured with precise equipment. Josephine herself loved cooking, but she never had the patience for these tartes, which appeared to be such an integral part of rural Dordogne life. Her efforts were still delicious, but they did not have the same aesthetic appearance with the fruit, thickly sliced and randomly placed. She would never have dared produce one of her more individual creations at such an important occasion.

As the sun began to slip from the sky and the afternoon to cool, the meal continued. The children, who rose and returned to the table like hens pecking at corn, played their games of catch on the lawns of the castle, reminding Josephine of her own yearnings. A child of her own. She glanced again at Jack. She thought him a suitable father if ever there was one. Yet like so many other things, that would have to wait until after the war was over.

An impressive array of local cheese followed the dessert, goats cheese from the farm at Castelnaud, Perail de Brebis from Beynac, and some Roquefort, which Jack had managed to acquire at the market in Sarlat, were all the more delicious for the accompanying freshly baked bread. As they sipped wine, dusk slipped into evening. It was impossible to believe how recently she had left Paris. The warm summer days, the wine and the slow pace of rural life were curiously seductive. Here in the depths of the Périgord, she sensed the ease with which one could forget the war, forget the persecution of the Jews, forget everything important. Why, she could even forget she was black. Life could be so perfect, she thought, if there were more days like this, if only people could learn to live together peacefully.

On est bien ici. How many times had she heard the phrase? Yes, life in the southwest of France was good. Money did not count for much, and peasants lived like kings. Not that she considered her rural neighbors as peasants. Further down the table, Madame Soubou sipped her wine and talked enthusiastically about methods of storing apples. Wrinkled and weathered, her brown face was animated and passionate, belying her eighty-five years. Josephine had often watched her wiry frame working in the fields, tossing hay and leading the goats for milking. The woman appeared as ageless as the hills and valleys that surrounded her homeland. It was comforting to know that life had continued like this for centuries,

but she would not allow herself to be lulled into a false sense of security.

This rural existence might be a world apart from the sophistication and elegance of Paris life, but the Hitlerite threat was no less real. There might not be any immediate need for gas masks and blackout curtains in the heart of Dordogne, but her heart burned with anger as she pictured the Nazi marches through her beloved Paris. All too clearly, she could see the scarlet red banners emblazoned with black swastikas lining the Rue Rivoli.

Even as she watched the faces around the table, the shadow of wars, both this one and the Great War, had touched them all. She, as a Jew and Negro, who according to the signs at every train station along the demarcation line, was no longer welcome in her beloved Paris. Jack, who was as loyal and brave a Frenchman as one could hope to find, was now a traitor on the run from the Vichy regime.

It was the winds of war that had blown their fellow refugees to Milandes. Emmanuel Bayonne, a sailor from the French Navy, had deserted on the day of the armistice; Joseph Boue, a high-ranking pilot, had deserted from the Air Force on the same day; Francois, a Polish refugee, had fled Poland on the day of the Nazi invasion; and Monsieur and Madame Jacob, Jewish refugees from Belgium, had been rescued by Josephine at the shelter.

Even the local villagers of this remote corner, whose origins were French from the very beginnings of time, had not escaped. Malaurie had wept when the armistice was declared and imagined he was attacking Nazis with every strike to his anvil as he worked in his blacksmith's forge next to the chateau.

Monsieur and Madame Laremie worried about the safety of their two sons who were captured at Dunkirk and were now in a prisoner of war camp in Germany. Madame Souberon had lost her husband at Verdun in the Great War, and now her only daughter was trapped in the Occupied Zone.

Even their national holiday had been abolished by Nazi edict.

Nonetheless, Josephine had been determined to celebrate the Fourteenth of July. Was not Milandes her kingdom? So, they kept French time and declared a holiday. Ration cards had been saved in preparation. Bastille Day was a celebration of the day when the peasants had risen up to protest against their oppressors. The day they had stormed the Bastille in Paris. The day that the French Revolution was born together with the fundamental principles of the French constitution: Liberty, Equality, Fraternity. Hitler and his policies of racial hatred and division had no place in her kingdom. The celebration would serve as a symbol of hope. France might have agreed to a humiliating armistice. Two-and-a-half million Frenchmen might be in German prisoner of war camps. SS troops might march along the Champs-Élysées every day. France might have lost the battle, but she had not lost the war. General de Gaulle's call to arms had given hope where there was humiliation. His words were the spark from which a great fire would grow. An inferno which would burn to ashes the Nazi dream of a Reich which would endure for a thousand years.

Jack took her hand and pulled her onto the lawn. She could not resist and molded to his body as they danced a slow foxtrot to the strains of a jazz record that drifted faintly from the drawing room. After the singing and dancing, which typically would last well into the early hours of the morning, perhaps even until the dawn light as beams of sunlight sneaked through her bedroom window, they would make love passionately in her bed, oblivious to everything but each other's touch.

She sniffed his neck, enjoying the faint scent of aftershave. In his arms, her Foxy's arms, she felt safe. She had never felt like that before. It was unsettling. She did not know if she should allow herself to get used to it. Her heart tightened. If she became accustomed to Jack's protection, to having him around, to needing him even, what then?

Chapter 19

MILANDES, EARLY
SEPTEMBER 1940

Josephine was already up, wiggling her *derriere* to tantalize him as she leaned over the windowsill. He admired her naked body as she chattered enthusiastically. "It's beautiful today. Let's get the skiffs and take a picnic. We have to make the most of the time here. It breaks my heart to be leaving, but we must get to London. How soon do you think we will have word?"

Jack nipped her nose to tease her. "Patience, chérie, patience. As soon as we receive instructions from the resistance." "Oh, Jack," she threw herself down on the bed. "Sometimes I wish we could stay here and have children and forget about the war." "Me too, chérie. And we could here." He sighed and gazed up at the vaulted ceiling of her bedroom. The chateau had stood in its defensive hilltop position, guarding the Dordogne Valley for centuries. It could withstand a Nazi invasion. Although, by luck, they had found themselves within Vichy France, it became more and more apparent that the Vichy Government was little more than a puppet of the Nazis. How many French had decided to accept the hand offered in friendship by Germany, like the children in Paris accepting the sweets and bananas offered by German soldiers? How easy it would be in the rural backwater that was the Dordogne to ignore the rumors of atrocities and concentrate only on daily life. The grapes still needed to be gathered, the hay still needed to be harvested, the apples hung patiently on the trees waiting to be picked. The foie gras still tasted delicious and the pear *eau de vie* still burned the back of the throat. Would it be so difficult to forget about London, about the Free French Forces, about the death warrant on his head?

Jack wondered whether he should try to persuade Josephine to give up her dream of joining the Free French Forces, persuade her to forget General de Gaulle. He had a duty to her too, did he not? He loved France, but he loved her too.

Any thorough search of the chateau would inevitably result in Josephine's arrest. Jack's stomach turned. The thought of her subjected to humiliation and torture was abhorrent. That it should arise as a result of his allowing her to continue their dangerous game was unthinkable.

"Josephine, perhaps I should go to London alone."

Her expression turned from one of animation to one of hurt. "What do you mean? We have both been accepted into the Free French Forces, that's what you told me."

"Yes, it's true, but haven't you done enough? You know the risks are enormous. If you are betrayed and handed over to the Nazis ... A search of this place could reveal enough for you to end up before a firing squad. They won't treat you any differently because you are a woman or famous."

She laughed. "I have no illusions about how they would treat me." She held out her arms. "I'm black and married to a Jew. But I won't let them beat me. I won't let them turn Paris into a pit where their evil festers. I still remember when I arrived in Paris," she said dancing round the room, "I was nineteen years old, and it was the first time in my life I could sit in a restaurant and eat with white people. The first time I could drink champagne. The first time I could kiss a white man in public." She leaned across planting a kiss on his lips. "Do you think I will let Hitler take that away from me? I will fight any way I can." She twirled round again. "And I haven't done too badly, have I?"

He nodded. It was indisputable that she had excelled as an 'honorable correspondent.' The information she had obtained had been of vital importance, and their next mission, which Paillole had hinted at, promised to be of even more significance.

"Jack, we don't know what's going to happen, whether we will have much more time together. We spend our life in limbo. Let's pretend, just for today, that the war isn't happening. Let's pretend that there is no rationing. That Madame Laborie's boys have been released and are working in the fields. Let's pretend that we are on our honeymoon.

I'll get Paulette to prepare a picnic. I know there is some foie gras, the hunters have left some venison and there is plenty of fruit. There is wine, of course, and we can take fresh bread. It will be a feast."

Jack nodded. "We could row down the river, maybe stop in Saint-Cyprien and have an apéro at Madeleine's before we come back."

"Of course, that would be perfect. After all, there is nothing suspicious about my being visited by my ballet instructor, what's more there is nothing suspicious about Josephine Baker being seen with a handsome young man indeed..." she gave a mischievous giggle, ..."it would be extremely suspicious if she was seen without a handsome young man. What do you think?" She twirled into his arms and threw her arms around his neck.

"I don't think I know how to refuse you." He laughed, bending down to kiss her.

They walked down the narrow path which threaded its way through the giant oaks that covered the hillside. The sun was shining, and the only sounds were birds singing and the distant lowing of some cows pasturing in the valley.

They neared the boathouse, and Jack pulled out the skiffs. Soon they were on the river following the current as it wound its way languorously downstream.

Cliffs towered above them on either side of the river; the chateau at Beynac glided past. As always, Jack was in awe of the majestic beauty of the historic area which some called the cradle of civilization. A jewel hidden in rural France.

· · ·

As always, Josephine's fascination for the area and for the chateau of Milandes intrigued him. It was as far from the life she had enjoyed in Paris during *les Années folles* as one could imagine. Yet there were so many aspects to her character. She was like one of her multifaceted diamonds. One moment, she was the girl who could dance and party for eighteen hours or more a day; another, the temptress with countless lovers; another, the woman who longed for a child. With her vicious temper, she could instill terror in anyone who crossed her or did not meet her exacting standards, but paradoxically, she was also the good Samaritan, extravagantly generous when her heart was touched. She was all these things and more, including the fearless spy who thought nothing of risking her life for a country that was not even her own.

Jack leaned back in his skiff enjoying the warm sun on his face. Josephine, powering ahead, shouted at him to hurry up or he would have to buy the drinks. He smiled. He could happily spend a lifetime getting to know this crazy woman. With her there was only one certainty, life would never be dull.

Chapter 20

MILANDES, MID-SEPT 1940

"Madame, there is a young man at the door. He insists on seeing you. He refused to give his name; he says it is of no consequence. You do not know him."

Josephine glanced up from her desk. Paulette was usually expert at averting unexpected visitors without disturbing her.

"I'm busy," she said, lifting up the stack of letters.

"Madame, he won't go away."

"What's it about?"

"He says he can't tell me, but that it is a matter of the utmost importance – and secrecy. He can only speak to you."

Josephine brightened. "A mystery. That is more interesting. Is he handsome?"

Paulette looked disapproving. "Madame ..."

Josephine laughed. "It's more entertaining to waste one's time with a handsome young man rather than a boring old one, is it not?" She rolled her eyes expressively and grinned at Paulette.

"It's true, isn't it?" she added teasingly. "And he is handsome. I can tell by your expression."

Paulette gave an exasperated grunt.

"So, you see, the question is an important one. Well if this handsome young man needs to see me desperately, I mustn't keep him waiting. Take him through to the library. I will see him there...and get Jack."

Josephine settled in an armchair beside the carved stone fireplace and turned towards the doorway so she could study her unexpected visitor from the moment of his arrival.

The young man was strikingly good-looking, as she had guessed, not tall but tanned with dark hair and soulful brown eyes. He wore a dark jacket and boots, in a style typical of the young men of the area, although with the threatened Young Workers Scheme, mobilization and work programs, fit young men had become scarce on the ground.

She watched his face intently as he entered the room. Was there a reluctance to engage his eyes with her? Some men were like that, if they felt intimidated by her fame. Perhaps it was the opulence of the room which unsettled him.

She gestured for him to take the chair opposite her.

He ignored it and came to stand directly in front of her.

"Mademoiselle," he gave a little bow. "Please forgive my insistence on seeing you. I do not wish you to think me impertinent, but I have information which is of the utmost importance. I need your help." He took a worn leather satchel from under his arm and began in a rather clumsy way to open the catch. Meantime, he continued to speak, "I need you to give these documents to the French Secret Service." He glanced at her for a moment just failing to catch her eye before rushing on. "I will have more in a week, then I need help to get to England."

He had taken a sheaf of papers from the case, which he fluttered before her eyes. She glimpsed what appeared to be photographs and maps interspersed between the typewritten pages.

His words whirred around in her head. *Information of the utmost importance. French Secret Service.*

Her eyes locked onto the papers fanning before her eyes. Vital information or a trap? Her heart raced as she struggled to remain calm. Friend or foe? Resistant or double agent?

She had only a moment to decide. Her life and that of her fellow residents at the chateau depended upon her decision.

She raised her hands, palms upwards.

"Stop there, please." She stood up, indicating that the meeting was over. Her voice was firm.

"I'm sorry, but you've made a mistake. I have no idea what you are talking about. While I wish you good luck in travelling to England, if that is what you want, I have no contacts or means of helping you get there. I am an artiste," she emphasized the word with a hand over her chest. "All I care about is my art."

She was relieved to notice Jack slip into the room. Then she turned to the young man. "Now if you'll excuse me, I have matters to attend to. This is Jack Saunders; you can talk to him as if he were me."

"It can't be true," the young man exclaimed, as he looked from Josephine to Jack. "I know that I have not made a mistake. It's not possible." His voice cracked with despair. "The man who sent me here would never have done so if he had not been certain you would help."

"Who was it that sent you here?" Jack demanded.

"Father Dillard. You must know him. He is at Vichy."

"Never heard of him."

"But you must know him. Mademoiselle Baker must know him," the young man insisted.

"Father Dillard told me, go to Castelnaud – Beynac, near Sarlat. Ask for the Chateau des Milandes. There you will find the dancer Josephine Baker. Ask her.

He told me to stay at the chateau until it was time for me to leave for England."

Jack was withering in his scorn. "A likely story! This Father Dillard told you to stay here? Very generous of him." He folded his arms, carefully studying every movement and expression on the young man's face.

"You ..." the young looked at Jack. Desperation clear on his face, "have the accent of an Englishman. You must be able to help me."

"Calm down," Jack barked at him. "I understand you are

passionate about your cause, but I am not English. I am an American and completely indifferent to your war. Like Mademoiselle Baker, I am an artist. We have no interest in fighting in Europe, beyond hoping that it is all over soon and there is an end to this damned rationing, petrol shortages and travel restrictions. It's so damned inconvenient. Keep your papers. We have no interest in your conflict."

"But I want to join de Gaulle. For the last three weeks, I have tried to find a contact to help me. I don't want to arrive in England empty-handed. I want to prove my support is genuine. I have here ..." He reached into his case taking out the papers again. "Aviation code books for the German Air Force. They are genuine. It is vital that I get them to our friends in London."

"Look. I've told you. You're mistaken. We have no friends in London. Forget you ever came here. You are welcome to have a cup of tea and some eggs and bacon in the kitchen, then be on your way. There's a train this evening at six. If you miss that, the next one is not until tomorrow. Now, I have fish to catch. It is a day for fishing not listening to this nonsense. I will show you to the kitchen on my way out. Paulette, see that this young man has something to eat before he leaves."

Jack walked down to the river. He took his skiff and set out on the water with the intention of forgetting about the young man. Fish flitted alongside the craft, clearly visible in the water, as if they were deliberately taunting him. But the young man's insistent voice kept echoing in his mind. He had seemed so passionate. His eyes had radiated with sincerity, yet Jack had never heard of a Father Dillard, and any code books for the Luftwaffe would have the highest level of security. How could that young man have them in his possession if he was not a German spy? For once, the Dordogne River replete with fish could not divert Jack – he could not put the unexpected visitor out of his mind.

What if he had been genuine? What if those papers in his brief-case really did contain vital information useful to the Free French Forces?

About three that afternoon while Josephine and Jack were

relaxing in the dining room after a typical Périgordine lunch of goat's cheese salad with a generous serving of red wine, the doorbell of the chateau rang.

Paulette came to them. "Madame, it's German officers. I saw them pull up in their jeep. I was too frightened to answer."

The couple looked at each other. It was unusual but not unheard of for German soldiers to drift across the border from the Occupied zone. They were hiding illegal guns and outlawed radio equipment to say nothing of the French airman and sailor, Belgian Jews and a Polish refugee. They could all be shot if the chateau was searched.

Josephine was outwardly calm. "I'll go." She put down her glass of brandy and stood up. "You see to everything else."

As the ancient door swung slowly open Josephine appeared framed in the doorway, composed and radiant as if about to commence a stage performance. Before her a uniformed German officer. Josephine's eyes were drawn to the revolver in his holster and to the machine gun held by the soldier behind him. These two were flanked by three men in long leather coats and trilby hats.

The officer clicked his heels together and saluted. "Mademoiselle, excuse our intrusion. I am the area officer commissioned in respect of the Armistice. One of my duties is to control the surrender of arms in the Zone Libre. I have had occasion as a result of my duties to visit other chateaux in the district and I have to say ..." He paused for a moment admiring the outstanding views over the sweeping gardens and the Dordogne Valley beyond. "Yours is magnificent."

Josephine smiled radiantly at the officer. "Why don't you come in?"

The officer signaled rapidly with his hands and his subordinates took up positions guarding the ground floor entrances to the chateau. Josephine led the officer to the library. He sat down opposite her.

"Mademoiselle, it is a great pleasure to meet you in person," he said politely, as he removed his hat. But Josephine was conscious of the icy tone of his voice and the coldness in his eyes as they scanned the room as if already conducting an intensive search.

"Mademoiselle, you appreciate that my duties can at times be unpleasant." he said in a conversational tone.

Josephine could feel beads of sweat run down her back as the officer's intense blue eyes focused their piercing stare on her as he watched her features intently.

Calling on all her years of acting experience, Josephine lifted her hands and smiled, mustering all her charm. "This war is very unpleasant. As you know, I am American. I have no interest in it."

"You are married to a Jew, are you not?" the officer interrupted sharply.

"And soon we shall be divorced," Josephine replied equally sharply.

"I am charged with ensuring that all unauthorized weapons are surrendered. It is, you understand, a very serious offence to retain guns."

"Of course." Josephine nodded.

"Mademoiselle, I have heard reports that you hide weapons here." He stared intently at her. "What do you say to that?"

Josephine burst out laughing. "Why, officer, I hope you are not talking seriously. It is true that my grandparents were Red Indians, but it's a long time now since they gave up war and smoked the pipe of peace. While I can still remember the steps for a war dance, that's as close as I will get to fighting. I have no interest in this European war. I am American born. An artiste. All I care about is my art."

The officer stared at her in silence for what seemed like an eternity. At last, he stood up and put on his hat. "Very well, mademoiselle. I will not take up more of your time. I hope we do not meet in less congenial circumstances."

Josephine showed him to the door. The officer left, signaling to his subordinates who immediately followed him into the jeep. She watched them drive out through the entrance gates. She closed the door and collapsed against it.

The others crowded around her.

"We must leave as soon as possible. I can't go through that again," she exclaimed. "Having him here in my home. Sitting in my chair.

Talking like we were old friends. I felt as if I was going to vomit. But I did good, Jack, didn't I?"

"Yes, but they won't have been fooled," he answered.

"That young man must have been sent by them. It's too much of a coincidence that he should arrive first and then we have an investigation on the same day. Those documents he had must have been false as we suspected. Now they will know that they are dealing with professionals. An amateur would have fallen for their subterfuge. You did well, Josephine, but this means our cover is blown. All of us." He glanced round at everyone.

"We will have to leave here as soon as possible. They might just have been more careful because of Josephine's fame and American birth. I fear someone less well-known would have suffered a different fate."

As they sat around the kitchen table in order to formulate a plan, Jack thumped his fist on the wooden table and stood up.

"I can't forget the expression on that young man's face when we told him we couldn't help him. The way I see it, either he was an agent sent by the Germans, in which case we must stop all resistance activity immediately and hope they will eventually stop surveillance on the chateau, so we can resume business as normal. Or alternatively, he was genuine and was in possession of important documents which must be sent to England urgently. He took an enormous risk

contacting us. At the end of the day I'm scheduled to leave for England shortly. I could easily take some additional papers in my luggage." Jack thumped his hand on the table again. "Damn it. I'm going to telephone the police commissioner at Sarlat, Monsieur Ruffel. He is a decent man, a Gaullist and a man of action. He might be able to shed some light on this problem," Jack continued. "It is a risk, but I can't take the chance that this morning's visitor needs our help."

The others nodded their agreement, and in no time at all Monsieur Ruffel had joined them around the kitchen table with a cup of ersatz coffee. They agreed a course of action.

At six that evening, Jack and Monsieur Ruffel walked into the train station at Chastelnaud. There was no sign of the young man. The train pulled into the station, stopped briefly and then left in a cloud of steam without a trace of him. If he was headed for Vichy, in all likelihood he would have to catch the train at Siorac, so with due speed, Jack and Ruffel headed there. As they were getting out of the police car in Siorac, Jack spied the young man outside a café. He recognized them and disappeared inside. Jack and the police chief followed at pace. When they entered the café, the young man was already seated and intent upon a newspaper he appeared to have taken from a selection on the counter. He did not look up even as they approached.

"Police. Follow me."

The young man got up, picked up his coat and followed them.

"Get in."

Jack sat in the back beside the young man.

"Give me the documents."

"Impossible. I don't have them anymore."

"Where are they?"

"I threw them away."

"Where?"

"Near the chateau."

"Driver, the chateau...and hurry," Jack ordered.

The car braked sharply, and after a U-turn, the engine revved as the driver raced along the empty twisting road towards Milandes. The passengers travelled in suspenseful silence. The magnificent cliffs that flanked the Dordogne River watched as they had since the beginning of time.

As the silence became increasingly oppressive, Jack proffered the young man a cigarette.

He took it and smoked it calmly in silence.

Eventually, Jack asked, "What is your name?"

"La Besnerais."

"Your father is the Director of SNCF?" interjected the police commissioner.

"He is my uncle."

The police commissioner muttered barely audibly, "Nephew of La Besnerais a spy? It is not possible."

Jack kept up the pressure. "You understand that the consequences are serious if you do not speak truthfully. To put you at ease, I am going to tell you that I lied to you this morning. I am not an American. I am, in fact, an army officer on leave as a result of the armistice."

"Mon Dieu! Then turn around. When I saw you, I thought I had better get rid of the documents. I haven't thrown them away. I slid them under the table in the bistro where you apprehended me. You will find them there, but quickly. They are very important."

"Driver, Sarlat," the police commissioner ordered. The passengers were thrown about their seats as the car made another rapid direction change and sped off along the road towards Sarlat.

As soon as they reached the police station in Sarlat, the commissioner made a quick call directing the local policeman to collect the documents and take them urgently to his office.

The men enjoyed an aperitif of *eau de vie de prune*, a specialty of the commissioner's wife, while they waited.

The commissioner let out a slow whistle as he leaned back in his chair after examining the papers.

"Well, they appear to be genuine. Radio messages intercepted from the Luftwaffe which have not yet been decoded. The photographs and plans appear to provide comprehensive details of German air bases in the Occupied Zone. Well done, young man."

Jack scooped up the documentation and placed it in the satchel. "Don't worry," he patted the case. "I'll be able to find a home for this."

The commissioner gave them each a refill. "To the liberation." They toasted in unison before gulping the strong liqueur and slamming their glasses down on the wooden desk.

Chapter 21

MILANDES, OCTOBER 1940

"Please, you must," he said, holding out the papers. She laughed. She took the documentation from his hands and studied it for a moment. Identity papers on which her photograph was superimposed. She twisted her body round emulating the expression in the photograph and laughed. "Do I look like Emile Dumas?" Her eyes changed from flirtatiously provocative to angry.

"You have to get out of France," Jack retorted. "The Vichy Government is just a tool for the Germans. You heard Pétain's broadcast. His plea for collaboration. No more Liberty, Equality, Fraternity. Now it's Work, Family, Country...for God's sake, Josephine, they are building an internment camp just down the road. Being married to a Jew might just be enough to get you deported. There will be a record of you converting to Judaism somewhere. What if they find it?"

"I can't, Jack. I'm sorry. Can't you see? I can only be me. Josephine Baker does not creep through the undergrowth in a borrowed coat. She does not hide in the guise of a maid from Perigueux. She is unmistakable." In a theatrical move, she tossed the forged papers in the air and extended her arms as if taking an ovation from a throng.

"It's too dangerous now. We know the Vichy Police are suspicious. Your work as an 'honorable correspondent' has been admirable. You have achieved far more than we ever envisaged possible, but you must stop now. It's madness to continue."

"I told you at the start. France gave me life. Now I am ready to give my life for France."

"No, you have done enough already. Please, Josephine, you must leave here. I will be responsible forever if anything happens to you. I could not bear it." His voice cracked with emotion and he bent on his knee before her and kissed her hand.

It was the most perfect speech. One she could have imagined in one of her childhood plays. If only she'd had a hero then. But now they were grown. This was not a play, and she had made a promise that she was not prepared to break. Not for anyone. Not even for Jack, no matter how much he might beg her.

"I won't. I made a commitment. I won't stop. Not while there are Nazis in France."

"Please. You have done enough. More than most. Please go back to America while you still can. You will be safe."

"But I wouldn't be me. My place is here."

Jack became more agitated. "Your fame won't save you. If you are caught, you will be shot, beheaded even. You know what happened in Bordeaux. I couldn't bear it. Please, for my sake, will you go back?"

"You forget," she tossed a fur over her shoulder, "I am no longer American. I am black and I am married to a Jew. You would have me leave. Run like a frightened Negro, more used to picking cotton than battling wits with the German Ambassador. So, you would have me, what?"

She approached him close and moved round his neck sniffing his aftershave with her nose. The sexual tension between them was as tangible as the odor she inhaled, but she didn't care about that. She cared about what she believed in and making it count.

Chapter 22

GEORGE V HOTEL, VICHY, NOVEMBER 1940

As soon as their car arrived on the steps of the chartreuse, Paillole appeared in the entrance and moved swiftly down the steps to open the car door for Josephine. He bowed and kissed her hand as she alighted from the vehicle before signaling for his assistant to park the car.

"Mademoiselle Baker, I would appreciate if I could prevail upon you to autograph a programme for me. It will only take a few moments. I have one inside."

Josephine smiled. "Of course, my pleasure," she said graciously. Paillole, gliding past the other guests, led her and Jack swiftly to into the library. He closed the door and turned the key, then gestured them to the armchairs situated by the impressive stone fireplace. He passed them each a brandy. "To Liberation," he said with passion.

Josephine and Jack raised their glasses.

"We don't have much time. I don't want to arouse the suspicions of the other guests. You have heard the news." They nodded. "You understand the implications. With de Gaulle declared a traitor by the Vichy Government and a death warrant issued for him, anyone answering his call to arms can expect the same fate."

Paillole turned to Josephine.

"You understand, mademoiselle, if you want to continue on the route you have chosen, tonight we will say goodbye for good to both Captain Abtey and Jack Saunders."

Josephine looked startled, glancing at Jack in confusion. Paillole continued more gently. "It is not too late for either of you to change your minds. You, captain, can still have a place in my organization should you choose to remain in the Zone Libre."

"No, my mind is made up."

"Then it appears likely you will be put on a list of those to be shot when captured. I have arrangements in place to furnish you with a new passport and identity papers. Here, he slipped a slip of paper across the table. Write down the name, address, occupation and date and place of birth you have chosen for your new identity. Remember you must be over forty. Now that I have the photographs, I can have the papers ready for you to collect tomorrow. Come back then and I will give you the identity papers and the intelligence which must be transported to London. I need to emphasize just how you would be treated were you to be caught with this information. You under-stand?" he gave Jack a serious look. Jack nodded.

Paillole glanced at the paper Jack had written on and turned to Josephine. "Meet your new dance choreographer, that is, if you are still determined to become a member of the Free French Forces." Josephine nodded. "I must warn you of the danger. You have already done so much for France. No one has the right to ask you to do this. Volunteers only."

"I have sworn not to dance in France until it is free of Nazi rule. If I cannot dance, I shall die. I will fight for the Freedom of France. I have decided to go to London with Jack and join de Gaulle. We still can?"

"Yes, he is expecting you. Congratulations to you both. Now ..." he said before downing his drink. "I have monopolized your time long enough." He took them both by the arm. "Good luck to you both. Now, we must join the other guests before we arouse suspicion."

· · ·

NEXT DAY

Josephine was tempted to ignore the gentle knock on her door. The soiree organized in her honor had lasted most of the night. She turned over sleepily in her bed, until she recognized Jack's distinctive tap. She leapt from the bed and flung open the door. A man wearing glasses and a neat moustache stood there. He was flamboyantly dressed with an audaciously vibrant silk cravat.

"Madame," he said taking a little bow, "let me introduce myself. Jacques François Hebert, born at Marseille on 16 September 1899, artiste by profession and residing normally at Toulouse, at your service."

"Jack," she screamed, dragging him into her bedroom. "I do like an older man, and the moustache makes you look quite distinguished. Even I didn't recognize you for a minute." She laughed and then exclaimed, "No one would believe you are the former Chief of Military Counter-Espionage in Paris."

"That's the whole idea."

Paillole tapped the briefcase as he spoke. "You must understand the implications of the task you are about to undertake. It is a matter of extreme urgency that these papers are taken to London. The Germans are winning the war. At the moment, all we can do is try and delay their victory. The British have sworn to continue the fight. We must give them every assistance possible. They fear an invasion is imminent. It is urgent that we put in place an effective system for exchange of information which will be to our mutual benefit.

"First of all, you must understand that this cooperation is of the utmost secrecy. If the Germans discover that elements of the Vichy Government are working against them, they will occupy the whole of France and no doubt take revenge on French soldiers imprisoned in Germany.

"Second, you must impress upon the British how much we will support them when the time comes. They must understand, however, that our support must be kept secret. The consequences will be horrific if our complicity is discovered."

Paillole opened the briefcase and spread out the documents on the table as he continued speaking, "Now, here is information which I am sure will reassure the British of our sincerity.

Details of Nazi bases located in the Occupied Zone, gathered at great personal risk by our operatives. You will need to transcribe them in code form or in invisible ink onto your documentation then destroy the originals. We also have details here of the positions of the principal German troops in the west of France and, even more importantly, details of the German spies destined for England. We also have details of airfields and the positions of their parachute regiments."

Paillole lifted some photographs before continuing, "These are vital. Photographs of barges the Germans intend to use to cross the Channel. You will have to find a way of carrying them. These are the most important, but as you can imagine, there are also the most difficult to disguise and the most incriminating if you are caught. I trust that your journey to Spain will be successful. You appear to be a perfect team, and I have every confidence that your mission will be successful."

"Thank you," Josephine exclaimed making no attempt to disguise the excitement in her voice. "Thank you so much." She hugged Paillole, who made no attempt to disguise his pleasure at the unexpected display of affection. Jack took the briefcase and shook his hand. He was in no doubt either about the importance of what they were about to do, or how dangerous it would be.

Chapter 23

NICE, FRANCE, NOVEMBER 1940

THE PORTUGUESE EMBASSY

The Ambassador bowed. "Mademoiselle Baker, we are honored that you have chosen to perform in our country, and I will do everything in my power to ensure that the travel visas which you require will be provided with every urgency, but what I can I do? Unfortunately, my hands are tied. I have to obtain permission from Lisbon and that will take a minimum of three weeks." He shrugged. "It is the times we live in, I'm afraid. You understand, Portugal is filled with people trying to escape Europe. Administration is necessary, even in times like these."

Josephine nodded, trying to keep her frustration in check. "If there is any other solution, please contact me urgently. I would be very disappointed if my performance has to be cancelled."

"And the people of Portugal also. Now, I'm afraid I have some urgent matters which require my attention. I hope that we will meet again." The Ambassador gave a polite bow.

She and Jack wandered along the esplanade and stared over the waves to the horizon while the sea lapped gently against the pillars of the quay. "What are we going to do?" she muttered. "There must be a way?"

"Three weeks." Jack sighed. "Perhaps I should go alone. Try to hire a boat."

"No, this is my mission too."

"It's *our* mission, but maybe this time I should go alone. I don't think there is any disguising you?"

"Wait a minute," Josephine said, her face brightening. "I know the Brazilian ambassador."

"Brazil? How's that going to help?"

"Come on. We should be able to get an appointment today, if we hurry."

NEXT DAY

Jack grinned as he picked up the documents Josephine had spread out on the table.

"How did you do it?"

Josephine glowed with pride as she explained.

"I informed the Brazilian Ambassador that I have a show I wish to perform in Brazil. It is ready. I had plans in place to go last year, but I had to cancel everything because of the war. I told him that the time is right for me to make the journey." Josephine laughed enjoying the puzzlement on Jack's face. She reached forward tweaking his nose. "To get to Brazil, it would be customary to travel through Spain and Portugal. I would need transit visas. And of course, I cannot perform a show just by myself. I have my entourage who must accompany me. *Et voilà*: the visas."

"So, we are going to Brazil?" Jack asked. Josephine smiled as she put her arms around his neck and gazed at him.

"Of course not. We don't *need* to go to Brazil. We just need to *plan* to go there. We have twelve days before we leave, so we can go back to Milandes."

"You're incorrigible," Jack muttered as he examined the papers. His blood ran cold as he read the annotation to his own visa. "Accompanying Josephine Baker." If he was exposed as a spy, the words marked would serve as a death warrant for Josephine.

Chapter 24

MILANDES, 24 NOVEMBER 1940

It was hard to leave. It was the end of a dream which had never quite managed to come to fruition despite the deep and sincere wishes of its protagonists. The car was packed. The goodbyes had been said. Now all that was needed was Jack. He was the driver after all. Josephine wandered down the pathway to the Dordogne. The route they had shared so many times together in the last few months. She had expected him to have returned already. For a moment she wondered if he had left without her, seeking to spare her the dangers of the life she seemed compelled to lead, yet although she feared he would not return, she knew in her heart that if he had been delayed it was only one of the tenacious fish of the river that had commanded his attention.

As she arrived at their private mooring, she sat on the bank and surveyed the river. In the distance to the north, she could see a skiff. The movements of the rower suggested it was Jack and she waved. Against the sun's rays she thought she saw a responding movement and so returned to her place on the bank.

In minutes, he was beside her pulling the skiff onto the bank, before storing it in the boat house and locking the door.

"Thank you," he said, bending to kiss her while he held up two fish. "That was the best leaving present ever." His eyes filled with emotion and she could see that leaving Milandes was as momentous for him as it was for her. He took her hands and kissed her again. "We will always have this place. We will fight for it, and we will come back here when the war is finished. When we have won."

"Yes, of course, Jack," she said, but she could not meet his eyes. Theirs was not the first dream that would crash and burn at Milandes.

Jack noticed her reticence. He caught hold of her arms and with his customary intuitiveness asked, "Tell me how you came to rent the place." She glanced away, but he pulled her back. "Tell me," he repeated, as though he knew it was important.

"Now is not the time," she answered curtly. "We must leave. The car is ready."

"No, Josephine, tell me."

"If you must know, I first noticed the castle while on holiday with Jean. We visited it and I rented it immediately. I wanted it to be our home for when we had children. We got married. I had a miscarriage. I could not bear to look at him again. Our dream ended here. Do you have any other questions?" Her voice was harsh now and distant.

Jack felt as if his heart had been gripped with an iron fist. Had he been only an understudy for Jean, a poor replacement? He looked into her eyes, filled with pain. He could see she loved him as deeply as he loved her. Their dream was real. He had to make her understand that. "Josephine," he said. His voice was so soft, so tender it could have seduced the coldest heart. "Our dream will begin here. It is a beginning not an ending." He kissed her hand with a tenderness which brought tears to her eyes. "We may be leaving today, but our future is here, together."

She grasped his hands and smiled and nodded, overcome with emotion. She knew he was right. They could make the future they had dreamed of together here, if only they could survive the war.

Chapter 25

PAU, FRANCE, 25 NOVEMBER 1940

They stood at the train station waiting together with all the other passengers. They were hungry. The station buffet had nothing on offer except bread and sardines. It looked particularly unappetizing. "Anything, Jack," said Josephine. He approached the counter but despite a roll of notes, returned empty-handed. "They are insisting on ration coupons," he explained. "I'm sorry."

"Perhaps it's a good thing," Josephine said with a wry smile. "They really don't look very good. Oh, look at those poor souls," she said nodding towards a crowd of people walking down towards the platform for the Siberian line. As the group came closer they could see that the crowd of perhaps one hundred people comprised old men, women and children. None amongst them looked fit for work. Josephine heard one of the railway station guards say that the group had been forced out by the Nazis, when they annexed Alsace and Moselle. Obliged to take only one suitcase. They had descended from cattle trucks which had transported them from their homes to the gates of the Pyrenees, the straw still clinging to their clothes. They saw an old man with stick legs supported by two rabbis as he struggled along. He was wearing an old army coat and his bag was a small rucksack containing his worldly possessions. Behind him, a young lad of about six carried a girl of about three on his back. They had a knitted shawl around their shoulders and no shoes – just sackcloth tied with string. Those less tired carried the bags of others. They all had deathly pale faces and worried expressions. It was a sight to break the heart. Jack clenched his fists. Josephine stroked his arm. What could they do? They had to get the documents to London.

While they watched, across the platform, the dispossessed were loaded onto another set of cattle trucks. Guards yelled orders impatiently. Dogs barked. The doors slammed shut and the train departed. Jack and Josephine found themselves the only passengers on their train as it arrived at the border, Canfranc. They each handed their passports to the customs officer. This was the first real test of Jack's identity papers. Would the official really believe he was over forty? Was he really going to be able to leave France?

The customs officer stopped, stared, paused, consulted a colleague and stared at them again. He was still holding their passports. Then in an excitable tone, he summoned the police. Jack and Josephine glanced at each other. Josephine felt her heart stop. Taking a deep breath, she smiled as the men swarmed towards her. French customs officials, Spanish customs officials, French and Spanish police. The chief of the whole border post. They all wanted to see Josephine, speak one word to her. The whole post erupted in excitement as if she had just performed and they wanted to demonstrate their appreciation.

Josephine charmed them with her usual intimate style. Jack kept a respectful distance, befitting his role. Finally, when the audience was satisfied, the train rolled on. The wheels turned through the night with reassuring rhythm, towards Portugal and their destiny. As soon as they arrived in Madrid, Jack attempted to make reservations for the onward train journey to Lisbon. The station was filled with people desperate to get out of Spain and there was no possibility of tickets for at least three days.

"Let's try the airport," Josephine suggested and they presented themselves at Barajas Airport. They were lucky. Through an unexpected cancellation, there were two seats available on a plane leaving in two hours, otherwise nothing for eight days. They purchased the tickets and waited.

Jack could feel his heart thumping each time their passports were handed to officials. This examination appeared to be taking longer than usual. The official studying the passport summoned his colleagues. Three men in black hats examined the passport. Jack's name, Jacques Herbert was written on a form and then meticulously consulted against a list of names. Jack knew that as Jacques Herbert had only existed for a matter of weeks that it would be an act of the very devil himself if his name appeared. Yet he could feel his chest pounding. The official smiled politely and handed over the passport. "Enjoy your trip, sir."

"Thank you," Jack replied with relief.

The Spanish airport could have been a Nazi airbase. Jack counted the planes, twelve, each emblazoned with a swastika waiting in a line, while around, like grey ants, mechanics in trench coats carried out their work. And the civilians who were their fellow passengers watched Josephine in awe as she played the star. Smiling and nodding, looking as relaxed as if she were sipping champagne at Milandes, Josephine took her seat on the airplane. A Franco fighter plane escorted them for the first forty or so kilometers of the flight, and then disappeared.

Chapter 26

LISBON

For the French fleeing their homeland, Lisbon was a nightmare. It was a holding cell rather than a haven. The city was filled with refugees of all descriptions desperate to escape mainland Europe and reach safety in South America, families who had snatched their few most important or valuable belongings and were trying to secure their own safety by whatever means possible. But Lisbon was flooded not only with refugees. There were tourists visiting for entertainment untroubled by the war in Europe. There were those who travelled alone, who chose not to speak of their personal circumstances, whose faces, although worn, seemed to shine with an inner light, idealists determined to fight for their cause. There were spies and double agents. Friends or enemies. Persons seeking to help or perhaps entrap. It was impossible to know, and a mistaken trust could prove fatal. Nazi sympathizers sauntered along the boulevards talking carelessly about imminent landings on British shores. For them the war was already won. As soon as Jack and Josephine arrived in the city, Josephine immediately became the focus of press attention. Playing the celebrity, she gave interviews and explained her plans to perform in South America.

Chapter 27

LISBON, 28 NOVEMBER 1940

Jack glanced behind him to make sure he was not being followed. Hat pulled low over his face, he slipped into the courtyard. While it was not damning for him to be visiting the British Embassy, Josephine had been there only days before to attend a banquet, he did not want to draw any unnecessary attention to himself. After all, Jacques Abtey, as Head of Counter-Espionage in Paris, was known to the Nazis who had many spies and watchers in a country, which while officially neutral, was a fascist dictatorship. If he was recognized, it would be disastrous.

His first meeting had been a success-

He had met his contact and explained that the French Intelligence service, now operating undercover in Vichy France, wished to demonstrate their good faith and set up formal channels to exchange information. That was, of course on the basis that the British were working towards the same goal. The return of French troops to their own soil to repel the Germans."

His contact assured him that Britain would keep fighting. That even although Germans had reached the Channel Islands and the British population was demoralized, they were determined to stop the Nazi advance. His contact had been excited by the quality of intelligence Jack had been able to provide and assured him that the information about German military strategy could prove invaluable. He had concluded the meeting by explaining he would telegraph London immediately to organize the transmission of this intelligence. Jack had left his hotel details, so he could be contacted once there was a response from Britain.

The days had passed interminably but finally Jack had received an invitation to return to the British Embassy.

He was met immediately and escorted to his contact's office, where he was greeted with a handshake. "Sit down," the attaché said. "I have excellent news. We have permission from the British Secret Service to liaise directly with you. Given the delicacy of the situation, you will be contacted by a representative who will be solely responsible for exchanging intelligence with you. The information which you supplied has proved invaluable. We want you and Josephine to return to France to put in place a channel of communication for continuing this exchange of intelligence."

Jack was taken aback. "But we have left France. We plan to go to London."

The attaché raised his arms. "All in good time, my friend. But I am sure you understand how vital it is for us to have up-to-date and reliable information from France. We are all fighting for the liberation of your country. You can make the most important contribution at the present time by returning to France. We will provide more specific and detailed instructions shortly. You will need to stay in Lisbon for perhaps two weeks, by then we should have everything

in place."

"But I take orders from de Gaulle..."

"And de Gaulle is in London. These *are* your orders. Return to your hotel and wait."

As he walked past the hotel where Josephine was staying, he could see a squad of journalists camped outside. Josephine had invited the press to a reception. As usual her smile seemed to charm everyone. "Yes, she was passing through Lisbon. Yes, she had an engagement in Rio, Brazil. Yes, she had sung at the front and she had seen many sad things. Yes, she had left Paris and not returned since it had been occupied. Yes, she did not like the Nazis."

Her visit to Lisbon coincided with a visit by King Carol of Romania and the city seemed to be in a permanent festive state. Josephine along with other eminent visitors was feted by the Embassies of Britain, France and Belgium.

"Dammit," Josephine exclaimed, tossing down the newspaper, which boasted her photograph on the front page, featuring her signature wide smile, gleaming white teeth and flirtatious eyes. "I was looking forward to visiting London again." She strolled over to the hotel balcony, glancing down at the press pack who had taken up residence on the street outside her hotel. "I can't stay here for two weeks. I can't even go out of the hotel. What use is that? I will go back to France straight away. I can get in touch with Paillole and help set up the communication structures they need."

"I don't want you to go back to France alone. It will be more dangerous than ever now."

"Nonsense. I have been in Lisbon for a performance. We are having some difficulties with the organization of the show in Rio de Janeiro, so I'll leave you here to sort things out while I return to Milandes. We won't be apart for long." She stroked his jaw tenderly.

1 December 1940
Lisbon Radio
Goodbye, Josephine. À bientôt.

Chapter 28

3 DECEMBER 1940

Jack stared at the headline. The train that Josephine had originally planned to take for her return to France had been bombed. Many casualties. Thank God she had finally decided to travel by plane. She would be in Milandes now. Safe, or as safe as anyone could be in the Vichy Zone.

He would have to amuse himself as best he could in Lisbon until he received his next set of instructions. During the day, he occupied himself maintaining his cover as Josephine's choreographer and general assistant by making phone calls to Brazil in connection with the proposed show there. The evenings he spent at the Casino Estoril, watching and being watched. The Casino was a meeting point for the transient wealthy people who gathered in Lisbon: those trying to buy their way to America, desperate fugitives searching for an escape route of any kind, tourists who seemed untouched by the war surrounding them, profiteers and spies, Nazi collaborators and Portuguese soldiers on leave. People with secrets. Jack knew that when people gambled and lost, it was difficult to maintain the masks they had adopted. The Casino was therefore an excellent observation point, somewhere he could continue his work. And it was there one evening that Jack recognized an old friend.

Hans Mussig was the most extraordinary man he'd ever met. They'd first crossed paths in 1938 in Paris. Mussig had arrived in a poor state of health, having escaped from some of the great prisons of Europe. He was the son of a wealthy German industrialist and had a staunch Nazi family background. He had even been a member of the Hitler Youth organization.

But as an adult, as a matter of conscience, he had left the Party. When he and Jacques had first met, Mussig had travelled through Italy, then Monte Carlo, England and Holland before arriving in France. Keeping just ahead of his Nazi pursuers. He had just forty-eight hours in which to obtain a visa to get out of France as his name had been circulated to the French Police and the Sûreté by the Nazi government who were insisting on his extradition. Jack had interviewed him when he was arrested for using a false passport. Mussig had explained his persecution by the Nazis and his hatred for them, then he had offered to work undercover for the French as a double agent. Jack had met him again by chance at the Dieuxième Bureau in Paris. It was a strange coincidence that their paths should cross again in Portugal. Jack was grateful to have someone he could trust for company but nothing could stop him worrying about Josephine.

Chapter 29

MARSEILLE 10TH DECEMBER

"Josephine," Paillole said with pleasure as he invited her to sit in the chair opposite his desk. "I had not expected to have the pleasure of your company on French soil so soon." He leaned forward, whispering, "Tell me your news. I can see by your expression that the visit has been a successful one."

"Yes," she answered with enthusiasm. "The British want to cooperate. Jack is waiting in Lisbon for instructions, and I have come back to set things in motion here."

"Excellent," Paillole exclaimed, leaning back in his chair. "As you know, the resistance movements here are very fragmented. With no common chain of command, it is difficult to coordinate action.

A direct route to a command post in Britain will be vital, especially when the time comes." Josephine nodded. All resistance preparations were focused on means of disrupting Nazi forces when the time came for France to rise up. She prayed that it would be soon.

"We will set up the necessary communication routes here," Paillole continued. "It will take a little while. Can you wait in Marseille?"

"I don't know. I was considering returning to Milandes."

"Have you considered the possibility of doing a few performances here in the South?"

Her voice choked with indignation. "No, certainly not. I swore not to sing in France while the Nazis were in occupation."

"Look, Josephine," Paillole said, as he walked to the front of his desk and sat on it beside her. "It's an excellent cover. Why not arrange a few performances here in Marseille? It means you are close at hand so we can provide you with the next set of documents we want transmitted to Britain. You might not want to sing while there are German forces in France, but it could be a means of getting our intelligence to Britain more quickly."

"Well," Josephine considered. "I'm sure I can arrange something."

"Excellent." He walked over to his filing cabinet and extracted two glasses and an almost full bottle of French brandy.

"Let us celebrate. To victory!" They toasted and then knocked back the brandy.

As she left Paillole's office, her mind was already racing with plans for a production. She went directly to the Theatre de l'Opéra to meet with the directors. They readily agreed, thrilled to have such a famous celebrity appearing at their theatre, to mount a production of *La Creole*. The production was useful not only as a cover but also as a means of providing funds for Josephine who could not access her capital, frozen in the Occupied Zone. By means of her persuasiveness, charisma, energy and determination she managed to source costumes, an orchestra and the necessary cast. The show was in place in ten days.

Chapter 30
LISBON

Jack continued his collaboration with the British. It had been decided to purchase a small commercial boat to facilitate the exchange of information, but the formalities of purchase took time, and Jack was becoming increasingly impatient. He spent the evenings at the Casino, and he and Mussig became the best of friends.

Typically, they would rest in their respective rooms till about eleven in the morning, then go to the beach and smoke and drink under the palms at the pier. They'd run and swim after lunch, and then siesta in preparation for an evening at the Casino and the intelligence- gathering which that involved.

The days passed slowly. Jack maintained the pretense of waiting to depart for Brazil, where he would make the necessary preparations for the arrival of Josephine.

One night in the Casino bar, he was having a quiet drink when he noticed one of his old comrades from the Dieuxiéme Bureau. They both pretended not to recognize each other, conscious of the risks of exposure. London was slow in responding. Identifying German agents at the Casino was amusing, but not important enough to keep Jack in Lisbon.

Mussig had been contacted by Nazi agents who tried to persuade him to return to Germany. "We have won the war. You are a true Aryan and can still render service for Germany. Hitler is a man of insight and compassion. He understands that people make mistakes and he will welcome you back."

"I prefer to stay here in my skin than be at the mercy of Hitler," he told them with a grimace.

He explained later to Jack. "I'll have to go to South America, I can see that things are closing in around me. I need to get out as soon as possible. If there's anything I can do for you in South America, do not hesitate."

At last, Jack received the instruction he had been waiting for. The authorization for the purchase of a small boat to make the journeys between Portugal and Morocco. The boat would be registered in Portugal and operated by French Secret Service personnel to facilitate arrangements for exchange of information between southern Portugal and Casablanca.

"You can go back to France. Spain had stopped granting transit visas for France but began again yesterday. Go and try the consulate tomorrow morning. If you can't get a visa there, we will find another way."

The British contact gave him £1,000 for his voyage and to get set up in Casablanca. As a final cherry on the top, he confirmed that Jack and Josephine would be members of the Free French Army.

Jack left Lisbon by plane for Spain. At the airport he took his seat on a British plane whose passengers seemed to include adolescents of a school trip and tourists.

At Seville, he found himself waiting. The scheduled plane did not arrive and as there were only fourteen passengers, they were told that other arrangements had been made.

When they were escorted to the runway, Jack could see that they were about to depart on a plane with a swastika emblem. He found himself seated next to a man with a scar down his face.

Many of the passengers were men with long overcoats and boots. Jack suspected they were wearing uniforms underneath, and he decided it was prudent to pass the journey as inconspicuously as possible. He leaned his head against the window and pretended to be asleep.

It was an emotional experience to set foot on French soil again. Jack had been troubled by memories of the people he had seen loaded onto cattle trucks in Pau and everywhere there was a heavy and tense atmosphere, fueled no doubt by rumors that a Nazi occupation of Vichy France was imminent. As he waited in Narbonne for his transport connection to Marseille, Jack was conscious of the deserted and darkened streets, despite the proximity of Christmas, and the furtive manner of the few pedestrians who flitted from one alley to another. Marseille was little different, except for the large posters on every notice board announcing the opening performance of *La Creole* starring Josephine Baker on 24 December 1940. Christmas Eve. He would be in the audience to watch on opening night.

Jack rose and clapped as the curtain fell for the final time. What a performance. As usual, Josephine had been outstanding. He glanced around at the faces of the other members of the audience in the packed theatre. They seemed to share his appreciation. Jack smiled as he listened to the applause. How little they realized they had just watched a cover operation organized and performed by one of the first ever members of the Free French Forces.

He slipped backstage and found his way to Josephine's dressing room. Her face lit up when she saw him, and he picked her up, twirling her around the cramped dressing room.

"A magnificent performance."

"Thank you." She hugged and kissed him. "Thank goodness you made it." She sat down. "Tell me everything."

"Everything is in place. We are going to be posted to Casablanca. We will have a small motorboat put at our disposal, and through that we will be able to transmit information to Lisbon."

Josephine reached out clasping his hands. "It's happening, Jack. The tide is starting to turn."

"When will you be free here? Our work is important, and I don't want to leave here without you."

"It will be another fifteen days before my contract here is finished. I hadn't expected you before the tenth of January. If you need to go on ahead to Morocco, I can follow you once I'm finished here."

"I will meet with Paillole as soon as possible to obtain his instructions. I expect..." The pounding at the dressing room door interrupted him. Josephine's attendance at the opening night party and Christmas celebrations was being demanded.

The next day, they saw Paillole, who was delighted. They were scheduled to leave France for Morocco in fifteen days. "We can use the time to prepare intelligence for transmission," Paillole explained.

Josephine arranged for her animals to be collected from Milandes and for presents to be taken to her friends there.

Chapter 31

MARSEILLE, 7 JANUARY 1941

Paillole stood up. "It seems that as a result of worsening relations between the Pétain and the Nazi government, it is only a matter of days before the whole of France is occupied. Our source suggests that it is only administrative matters which have delayed this occurrence." Josephine looked at Jack in dismay.

"We can't risk either of you being trapped in France. Your work is far too important. To that end, it is imperative that you get to North Africa. I have arranged safe passage for you and your entourage. There is a boat leaving Marseille for Algiers tomorrow. You must be on it. It may be the last one to leave," he added somberly.

"I have two more performances scheduled," Josephine added. "One in Montpellier and another in Beziers."

"They will have to proceed without their leading lady," Paillole said. "You must be on the boat tomorrow. I am sure I can leave you two to decide how best to arrange things with the opera."

Josephine coughed. "Well, I have been feeling rather unwell lately."

"That's the spirit," Paillole said. "Now I have some information for you to deliver to Lisbon. It's a rather circuitous route but more useful than holding the documents here indefinitely. Good luck."

Chapter 32

HOTEL ALETI ALGIERS,
JANUARY 1941

Knock, knock.

Josephine glanced at Jack apprehensively.

Knock, knock. Forceful. Insistent. Authoritarian. Not the discreet tap of one of the employees who glided along the hotel corridors like subservient ghosts, their sole purpose, to accommodate every whim of the exclusive clientele who frequented the most famous hotel in Algiers.

Knock, knock. Louder this time.

Josephine stood up, her eyes wide with alarm. Jack calmly slipped the sheet music back into his leather music case and twisted the catch closed, then emptied the invisible ink from his fountain pen into his aftershave bottle, screwed on the top and slipped the container into his jacket pocket.

"We're good," he whispered, as his eyes scanned the room for any evidence which might betray them. Josephine studied herself in front of the mirror. A twist of her hips and the hem of her skirt rose to just above her knee. She opened another button at her neck and the suit, which only moments before had seemed demure, assumed a jauntily sexy air. She was ready.

Knock, knock.

Whoever was out there was not going away.

As she swung open the door, she smiled radiantly, and her body curved naturally into a subtly alluring pose. The stern face of a uniformed official was transformed as his eyes fixed on the woman before him. His mouth fell open in slow motion. Seconds passed. Finally, as he regained an element of composure and reassumed his cloak of officialdom, he said, in clipped tones.

"You are Mademoiselle Baker?" The words were less accusatory than he had intended.

Jack stepped forward.

"And you are?"

"Police Inspector Deloitte of the Algiers Police. "

"Do you have identification, Inspector?" Jack inquired politely.

The inspector pulled a card from his jacket and passed it over. Jack studied it intently before returning it.

"Your business, sir?" he asked.

"I have instructions to detain Mademoiselle Baker in Algiers."

"But why?" Josephine asked, trying to sound casual despite her pounding heart. Could they have been betrayed?

"She must pay four hundred thousand francs to the Theatre de l'Opéra in Marseille, if she wants to leave Algiers."

"That is ridiculous," Jack exclaimed.

"Inspector," Josephine interrupted, using her most charming voice. "Please come in and sit down." She gestured to the table and chairs. "Let's discuss this matter civilly," she added persuasively. The inspector nodded, giving every indication of being completely in awe of Mademoiselle Baker.

"There has been a terrible mistake," Josephine explained as she sat down opposite the policeman. "I have been ill, very ill ..." She touched her throat lightly. "My doctor insisted that I could not perform in Marseille. He advised that I come here, to a warmer climate immediately. Why, we have the x-rays here." She turned to Jack, he nodded and began to leaf through his briefcase in search of the medical certificate and x-rays.

"I could not breathe, far less sing," she added expressively. "I explained the situation to Monsieur Dubois and Monsieur Romette, the directors of the theatre. They were very understanding and agreed that neither my voice nor my health should be put at risk. They released me from the contract. As it was, there were only a few performances I could not honor."

"That's correct," confirmed Jack, "I was involved in the negotiations. They were given an opportunity to examine the medical certificate and x-rays. You can see the shadow on her lung here," Jack continued, indicating a point on the x-ray. "Everything was resolved before we left Marseille."

The inspector shrugged. "I have the court papers here." He passed them to Jack, who shook his head as he read the terms of the summons.

"This is a disgrace." He passed the documents to Josephine.

She read down the statement of the claim. "And the damages alleged, four hundred thousand francs. All I can say inspector is that I am astonished. Why it was myself who organized the production, the costumes, everything. I was in Marseille. I wanted to help the theatre."

The inspector shrugged again.

"I regret, mademoiselle, I have my orders. You must give me your assurance that you will remain in Algiers until this matter is resolved."

"But inspector, I am expected in Morocco."

"Mademoiselle, I would not wish to have to take you into custody. The accommodation we have to offer is not comparable with this hotel. I cannot leave here unless I have your assurance that you will not attempt to leave Algiers. You must understand that no entry visa will be issued to allow you enter Morocco until this matter is resolved."

Josephine glanced at Jack. The rendezvous for delivery of the documents was already scheduled. It was urgent. There could be no further delay in their travel plans.

Jack nodded discreetly. Josephine turned to the inspector with a wide smile.

"Of course. As you wish."

The inspector stood up, bowed and left. Jack placed his finger over his mouth signaling silence. He walked over to the door and pulled it sharply open. There was no one there. Then he glanced down the corridor, first in one direction then another. It was empty. He closed the door.

"Damn them. I explained to them that it was a matter of national importance that you leave France. They agreed. Now this!"

"What are we going to do? Do you think we should just leave? There must be a way to get into Morocco."

"No, far too risky and suspicious. You would blow your cover. The artiste Mademoiselle Baker would simply wait patiently in Algiers until this minor irritation is resolved."

"But we don't have time, Jack," she stamped her foot.

"You're far too famous to travel without a visa. Haven't we been through this before. Look, everything has been done properly. You have the medical documentation proving you can't perform. Your departure was negotiated. I am a witness to that. Why the directors are acting like bastards is beyond me."

"But what are we going to do? We promised Paillole that we could do this. He's relying on us."

"Hopefully we can get the visas sorted out quickly."

Josephine rolled her eyes. "Here! Let's be honest, there's no hope of that. He said a week, minimum."

"I'm sure you can pull a few strings here and there," Jack joked encouragingly.

Josephine brightened as she began to consider which of her contacts was best equipped to expedite the particular matter in hand.

"If necessary, I can go on ahead to Casablanca," Jack said.

"But that's too dangerous. You, they might search."

"It's the only way. We have to get the intelligence through. It's too important to delay any longer. Anyway, I am still Jacques Herbert, what could be more natural than that I go on ahead to arrange your performances and organize the accommodation while you recuperate in Algiers? Remember, you are ill."

"D' you know what," Josephine said, picking up the telephone to summon a messenger from reception. "I was asked to perform for the Air Force. If I am going to be forced to extend my stay here for a few days, I'll be able to do it after all."

Jack pushed his finger on the telephone ending the call.

"You must cancel. It will only irritate the directors of Theatre de l'Opéra."

"Nonsense. They might have stopped me leaving Algiers, but they are not going to stop me singing!"

Chapter 33

CASABLANCA, JANUARY 1941

Jack peered through the plane window as the descent began. Below, the city of Casablanca spread out like a complex sandcastle inhabited with ants who moved continuously in a preordained and mysterious order.

His first port of call was the Portuguese Embassy. With Josephine's letter for the Consul General requesting a visa to permit her choreographer and general assistant to travel to Lisbon to organize her performances, Jack expected to obtain the necessary travel documents as a matter of routine. It was explained painstakingly to him by a bored official that such a visa required permission direct from Lisbon. Once the application had been submitted, a minimum of fifteen days would be required for a response. Incensed, Jack had pleaded for a request to be made by telegraph. The suggestion was met with polite but firm refusal. That was not how things were done.

There could be no deviation from official procedure –
even if he was acting on behalf of Josephine Baker.

Dispirited, he left the Embassy hoping Josephine would be able to accelerate matters when she arrived. It had been difficult to leave her in Algeria, but indications had been that the delay would be short. A matter of days.

There would eventually be a court case to resolve the claims by the Theatre de l'Opéra, but meantime a letter of caution from Josephine would allow the administrative wheels to turn sufficiently to enable the issue of the necessary entry visa for Morocco. There had been some fiery debate prior to his departure, but eventually Josephine had accepted that Jack should go ahead in the hope of avoiding further delays.

He chuckled as he remembered. Josephine might have joined the Free French Forces, but she clearly had no intention of deferring to his superior rank. Having liaised with his contact in Casablanca, all that could be done was wait. Wait for Josephine. Wait for his own visa. Wait for his next set of instructions.

It was his first visit to Morocco and to Casablanca. With time on his hands, he resolved to use the opportunity afforded to explore the city. Once he set foot in the old town, the expectations he had created in his mind crumbled into ashes as surely as the documents he had burned after he had painstakingly transcribed and encoded them. He had expected the splendor and glamour of France's south coast, and Casablanca had those in abundance. There were exclusive hotels and beaches lined with palm trees, albeit that some were still under construction. There were airy cafés and a waterfront to rival that of Nice, Biarritz and even Cannes. But what Jack had not expected and had not prepared himself for was the mélange of civilization that was part of the very air one breathed in Casablanca.

To take one step into the medina was to take a step back in time, one thousand years or more. Life in the ancient city had changed little since it was built. A walk through the narrow alleyways, where typically Europeans only dared visit with local guides, was to wander through centuries and civilizations. Jews traded, gypsies told fortunes, Arabs bartered and, in the background, the melodic call to prayer from the minarets echoed through the medina.

It was there in Casablanca, while he waited for Josephine that Jack began to be seduced by the mystery that was Africa.

Jack pushed his way through the crowd at the train station, making his way to the first-class section of the train. He wanted to be able to open the carriage door for Josephine. Even as the train pulled to a stop in a final puff of steam, he could see her waving from the door. In a distinctive hat and white gloves, she looked effortlessly glamorous as always, despite the monkey draped around her neck. As he pulled the door open, Bonzo, the Great Dane, leapt on the platform with a welcoming woof and then Josephine alighted and hugged him. She was a vision of loveliness within the whirlwind of chaos surrounding her.

While the porters began unloading her cases, Jack fired instructions for their delivery to the hotel he had selected for her, together with the animals.

Then Josephine grabbed his arm and they walked purposefully along the railway platform. As soon as they were in their car, Josephine instructed the driver to take her to the Portuguese Embassy, impatient as ever, especially after two days of travel with her menagerie.

Jack trailed deferentially behind her as she swept into the building, maintaining his undercover role as her employee. At times, he found it infuriating, especially as Josephine seemed to enjoy altogether too much treating him like a lackey in public. He was provided with an uncomfortable wooden chair while he waited. He did not envy whoever was about to be the recipient of her anger regarding the delay.

Josephine was received immediately by the Ambassador. Jack's heart leapt when she emerged, smiling, thirty minutes later, waving a piece of paper which looked exactly like a travel visa. The Ambassador bowed, kissed her hand and effusively invited her to a reception that was scheduled for the following week. Once they were seated in their car, she took the document from her purse and handed it to him.

"I'm sorry, Jack," she said. "I really gave it to them about how much I needed you. Why I told them there would be no show without you, but he refused to grant a travel document for you."

Jack examined the document. Josephine's name was written neatly in copperplate at the top.

"I don't understand. If they can give you a visa straightaway, they can do the same for me."

She shrugged. "You saw yourself. I had him in my pocket. He said that because your application had already been submitted to Lisbon, he couldn't preempt any decision that might be made by his superiors. Makes sense, doesn't it?" Jack passed the document back to her.

"I'm sure it'll come through, and I know the Ambassador in Lisbon. I'll message him myself, just to make sure he knows how important you are. No show without Jack," she said. "Look, let's celebrate my getting here. I've had the journey from hell."

"Of course," Jack agreed, but he could not stop the feeling of unease in the pit of his stomach.

Chapter 34

TEN DAYS LATER

He slammed the door behind him with such force that the crystal glasses on the side table clinked together. Josephine, who had been wrapping one of her stage costumes, looked up startled.

"My visa has been refused again."

"Well, I'll have to go on alone with the documents."

"No," Jack retorted. "That's not an option. We'll have to postpone the mission until I can find a means of travel to Portugal."

"But there's no need. Everything's ready," she said, indicating the sheets of music spread across her desk. "The first performance is only a few days away. I can't delay any longer. The band is organized. I'll take the intelligence."

"No, I won't let you. It's too dangerous."

She looked at him with that look of hers, then with one hand on her hip, shaking the finger of her other hand, she said scornfully, "It's not your decision to make."

"You forget that I'm your superior officer."

Josephine raised an eyebrow. "Do you really want me to unleash my persuasive powers?" she asked in a sultry whisper.

He stood against the door, hands thrust in pockets, deep in thought. For a few moments, the room was completely silent.

There was a knock at the door, and then the maid entered carrying one of Josephine's evening gowns.

"Madame, this is the last one. The cars have been reserved."

Josephine nodded. "Good." She thanked the maid

before approaching Jack. "Look, I have concerts scheduled. I can't postpone. If I'm not in Lisbon, I'll have another writ, this time from Portugal. I have to go. You can follow as soon as the visa is granted. I'll try and sort it out from Lisbon."

"Well, go if you must, but without these," he said, taking the sheets of music they had prepared.

"No. I must take them."

"It would be madness."

"This information is vital; you know it is. Think how many lives it could save. We haven't had any trouble on any other trips. How many times have I done this now?" She made an elegant pose. "It seems that the scandalous Josephine Baker is above suspicion."

"But I've always been there."

"When your visa's granted, you can join me."

"You need a bodyguard. You've had no training. You don't even have a gun." He slid his revolver onto the table. "Will you take it? You know how to use it."

She laughed. "I'm Josephine Baker. I'm not going to carry a gun like that. It's not very elegant."

He came up close beside her and pressed the gun into her hands, closing her fingers around the handle. "Please, Josephine."

"No." Her voice was firm. She laid the gun back on the table.

Jack sat down, running his fingers through his hair.

"I don't know. I don't understand. Why no visa for me? I think they're suspicious. Perhaps they suspect that I'm an agent. I think that's why they've granted your visa and not mine."

"The die's cast then. If you're already under suspicion, it would be fatal if I called off the trip. That would really draw attention to us."

Jack nodded. He knew what she said was true, but to let her go alone, unprotected, scared him. She was an untrained agent, responsible for the transportation of compromising information, which, if discovered would

inevitably result in her being condemned as a spy.

Yet Josephine seemed unperturbed.

"Here, help me with this. We don't have much time."

Jack watched as she stepped elegantly out of her dress, revealing a matching cream-colored lacy camisole and brief set made especially for her by the couturières of Paris. She slipped the photographs from their hiding place in a secret compartment of her jewelry box and began to attach them to her underwear with safety pins. Jack felt his heart pound and his stomach churn. What if it was a trap? Josephine chattered and joked as she twisted and turned in front of the mirror, anxious that there should be no unseemly bumps in her clothing created by the documentation.

"I don't want people to think I am putting on weight," she said with a serious expression on her face. Jack took her face in his hands and kissed her tenderly on the lips.

"You are the most amazing woman I have ever met. I've said it before, and I'll say it again." And then he added silently to himself, "Until the day I die."

"Shhh." She disentangled herself from his arms. "I need to get ready."

Soon, they were interrupted by a knock at the door. "The taxi must be here."

Jack opened it and said, "We'll be along shortly. Tell everyone to load up."

He looked at Josephine. She was dressed for departure.

"How do I look?" She twisted and turned in her suit, completely oblivious to how sexy she looked with her long legs and high heels.

His eyes scrutinized her body for any sign of the concealed photographs. She had been right to be so careful, even the faintest line in her clothing could be enough to arouse the suspicion of a police officer or customs official. A search would without doubt prove fatal for the mission and in all likelihood for Josephine too.

"You must promise me to be careful."

"Yes, sir, Captain." She stood to attention.

He took her arms and squeezed them. "I don't want to let you go."

"You must. Don't you know there is a war on?"

"You know what to do."

She nodded.

"Once you get to Tangier, go to your hotel as arranged. A chambermaid will come to your room. If you think it is too risky to continue or if you think you are being followed, you give her the papers. The code phrase is 'Does Madam wish for her furs to be placed in the hotel storeroom?' Your response is, 'I always keep the ermine close.' And she will reply, 'Madam is very wise.' Then she will ask if you want to put the briefcase in the safe. If you believe you are under suspicion and it will be dangerous to continue, you must say, 'yes' in these circumstances and give her the case with all the music sheets and the photographs. When you collect the briefcase from the safe, it will have the music sheets inside, but the annotated version will have been removed. If you want to continue you say, 'No, I have some rehearsals and need to keep them with me.' You can still change your mind."

She shook her head.

"Remember, Josephine, if you have the slightest inkling that anyone is suspicious of you, you must get rid of the photographs. The music sheets are less compromising. You can say they are usually in my safeguard and the only reason you have them is because my visa was refused. That might be enough to save you. I do not believe that German Intelligence could be aware of your role. We have the highest-level of security. Only a handful of people know of your involvement. Even if the Nazis have figured out who I am, there is no reason to suspect your involvement. If, however, you are searched, there is no explaining the photographs. Promise me that you will get rid of them if there is even the slightest thing which doesn't seem quite as it should be. If the train is heavily guarded, you can close the curtains on your compartment. Take the photographs, throw them from the window. Promise me."

She nodded again.

"You understand that if the photographs are discovered in your possession, there is no saving you. Nothing will rescue you from a firing squad. Not your fame, not your American birth. Not being female. Nothing. Spain and Portugal might be neutral but they wouldn't hesitate to hand you over to the Germans if you are caught spying. The SS are ruthless. They show mercy to no one."

The train station was chaotic. They were late, but warned of their famous passenger, the train had delayed its departure. "We will make up the time en route," the stationmaster confided to Jack. The remaining passengers boarded the train. The whistle sounded signaling their imminent departure. Josephine turned to climb up the steps to her carriage. Jack held her back.

"I don't want you to go."

"I know, but I must." She unclenched his hands from her shoulders.

"I don't want to give you this, but I must." He reached deep into his jacket and pulled out a small red velvet covered box. He lifted it and pulled a ring from its socket. Josephine looked at him in puzzlement. She thought he had understood there could be no commitment, no promises, no future, not until the war had ended. He leaned close to her, shielding his movements from all round. He held the ring close to her and deftly pressed the side of the jewel. A catch flipped open to reveal a cavity. Inside a pill.

"Standard issue for agents in the field. It's a cyanide pill, quick, painless. It breaks my heart to give you this, but I can't bear the thought of you falling into the hands of the Gestapo. Their torture methods are fiendish. You understand."

She nodded. He flipped closed the hidden compartment and slipped the ring onto her finger.

"Wear it always. Promise me."

The guard approached and said politely, "Mademoiselle Baker, we must leave now."

Josephine nodded and boarded the train. She stood at the door as the guard slammed it closed. The train departed in clouds of steam.

Jack stood on the platform and watched the train chug down the line away from the station, away from him. Sadness swamped him. All he could do now was wait. And wonder. What if it was a trap?

Josephine slid the window closed and settled in her compartment. She was on her own now. No Jack. She felt frightened but exhilarated too. She was fighting for France in every sense. Her fingers ran over the new ring on her finger. She shuddered as she watched Vichy officers walk down the corridor. She pulled closed the curtains of her compartment. If she was lucky, she would be left alone for the journey. Ridiculous as it seemed, the first-class compartments were virtually empty while the poor travelled sitting on the roof and hanging from the railings at the tail end of the train.

As the train approached the border, she could feel her hands begin to tremble. She breathed deeply. It was a performance like any other. She would steal the show. As the train stopped at the border, she could hear the Spanish guards as they approached. She became increasingly conscious of the safely pins biting into her skin. She thought of Jack's apprehensive expression as the train had pulled out of the station. She had promised him she could do this. The compartment door slid open and she turned to the official with a dazzling smile. He stopped in his tracks. He barely glanced at her travel visa as he rummaged in his pockets for a piece of paper she could autograph.

Josephine sank back into the seat relaxed. Everything was running like clockwork. The train stopped again and Josephine could see the platform was filled with Spanish soldiers.

They flooded onto the train. As four officers entered her carriage, she concentrated on staring out the window. Her heart was racing as she remembered Jack's advice.

He had told her to destroy the photographs if she felt in

any way at risk. And how could she not when she experienced the intent stare of her travel companions. They won't dare, she repeated over and over to herself, trying to convince herself she was safe. But as she sat near them, she couldn't stop the fear rising through her body as insidious as a disease trying to poison her soul. Yet she was just as frightened to get up and walk past them in order to get rid of the incriminating evidence. Instead, she pretended to doze. She closed her eyes and leaned her head against the window as she strained to understand the men's conversation.

As the train pulled into Tangier, she was startled as one of the officers touched her arm. "Madame, we have arrived," he said politely. She smiled in response and then with relief as the men descended the train before her. Thank God, she thought, as she climbed down from her carriage onto the platform. Tangier, she had made it. Now for the long journey to Telouet and a reunion with her friend Thami El Glaoui, Lord of the Atlas and Pasha of Marrakesh. She felt exhilarated despite the long journey ahead. She had visited the Kasbah at Telouet before, and for her it symbolized all that she loved about Morocco. The palace, set high in the Atlas Mountains and accessed only by a perilous track, rose like a desert mirage from the red rocks of its surroundings. The Moorish architecture and intricate mosaics reminded her of the Tales of the Arabian Nights, which had inspired her childhood games. There she could become a princess from yesteryear as she wandered the corridors of the palace dressed in traditional robes. Her color faded and she could forget she was black. Or mixed race or whatever it was she was.

But there was danger too. The Pasha was a generous host and a charismatic companion, but also a man of his time. The centuries had done little to change the way of life in rural Morocco, and the Pasha lived and ruled in a manner not dissimilar to his predecessors. He was a warlord known for his ruthlessness towards his enemies. Rumors of his dungeons, filled with those who opposed him, rippled under the surface of polite conversation.

His family was governed with the same strict rules as applied to his subjects. His wives and concubines were confined in his harem, but on her visits, Josephine enjoyed unparalleled freedom, roaming the palace freely and dining with the men while the other women either served them with downcast eyes or watched silently from latticed galleries.

The Pasha was amongst the wealthiest men in the world, and his receptions were legendary. This one given in her honor was bound to be memorable, not only for its lavishness, but because amongst the guests there would be an abundance of opportunities for her favorite pastime – espionage.

Chapter 35

CASABLANCA, JANUARY 1941

Waiting, waiting. Jack joined the thousands of others waiting in Casablanca. Waiting for exit visas, waiting to be rescued, waiting for America to enter the war, waiting for something to happen. As he waited, he paced the streets, watching everyone and everything, eavesdropping on conversations in cafés and bars. The city had become a city of intrigue. A flood of European refugees had doubled the indigenous population of Arabs, Jews and French. Nazis, confident of their invincibility, swaggered the streets.

Partisans escaping Franco's retribution plotted in bars. Wealthy American tourists admired the architecture of the ancient minarets, seemingly unconscious of the war raging in Europe. He could feel eyes burrowing into his back as he paced the city. Spies everywhere. Watching. As did he. Searching always for traitors and fifth columnists, for suspicious behavior, for a word or a phrase out of place, anything that might reveal the true identity of the speaker. The tension was tangible in the air as everyone watched.

In the intense heat, each day seemed to pass more slowly than its predecessor. He found it unbearable. Not knowing what was happening to Josephine made the situation even worse.

Finally, he received a telegram from her:

. . .

VISA DIFFICULT – DON'T GIVE UP HOPE.

Jack scrunched up the strip of paper and threw it forcibly against the wall. He felt like he was in prison. He was, like so many others, trapped in Casablanca.

As he collected his key from hotel reception, he was handed a new telegram, but it was not from Josephine. That meant one thing: it was from his contact. He ran upstairs to his room, anxious to read the message in complete privacy. It had to be his instructions to leave. It had to be.

NO HOPE OF VISA – FURTHER INSTRUCTIONS TO FOLLOW

His fist pounded the table. He would not stay in Casablanca, waiting in this ungodly limbo like everyone else. He hadn't deserted the Deuxième Bureau for that. Stalking the beach as he stared out over the waves, he resolved to find a way to join Josephine in Lisbon. All that was needed was a boat. Surely, it would be possible to land on the Portuguese coast, he thought. He sent an urgent response to his order:

PERMISSION TO LAND BY BOAT.

The reply came weeks later:

REQUEST UNDER CONSIDERATION. WAIT AS SPECIAL PERMISSION REQUIRED.

. . .

Weeks passed. Jack sent another message indicating he wished to leave Casablanca. Had he not left France on the assurance that he could join the Free French in London?

SUCH A VOYAGE IS PREMATURE BECAUSE WE ARE UNABLE TO CONFIRM THAT A DISEMBARKATION IN PORTUGAL WILL TAKE PLACE IN FAVORABLE CONDITIONS. UNDER NO CIRCUMSTANCES JEOPARDIZE THE MISSION.

Jack could have wept when he read the note. He feared that he was to be left forgotten on the shore to pace the sands of Casablanca while Josephine risked life and limb to continue their work alone.

Jack looked-on, his curiosity aroused, as a sea of people formed as if from nowhere, filling the narrow street, rippling in one direction as though it were an ebbing tide. As he approached the clatter of voices, it was possible to discern words. Josephine ... Baker ... station. He joined the throng. As they neared the station, it became increasingly difficult to move, but he was determined. Finally, he could see her. Bouquet of flowers in hand, smiling radiantly. She was welcomed by an official and led to a waiting taxi.

He turned and made his way to her hotel. Once there, he alerted the staff to her imminent arrival, and then poured himself a glass of bourbon and sat down in the armchair to wait patiently. If the reception at the train station was anything to go by, it would be some time before she was free of the press who had been accumulating outside the hotel even as he arrived.

Eventually she swept through the door and into his arms. "Chérie," he murmured as he ran his fingers down the sides of her face. "You are more beautiful each time I see you."

She laughed with pleasure at his compliment. Tracing her finger under his chin, she teased, "You did not forget me? I can be very jealous you know."

Jack pulled her towards him and kissed her deeply. He could not ignore how intense his feelings of love had become. They were obliged to keep their relationship secret. To maintain an emotional distance from each other because of their circumstances. If either was unveiled as a spy, knowledge of their intimacy could endanger the other. Josephine's hands ran down his body. They had been apart for so long, now was a time for love.

It was some hours later before Josephine was ready to recount her adventures.

"When I arrived in Tangier, I was welcomed by friends of the Pasha, Abderahman Menebhi, who is related to the Sultan of French Morocco, and Ahmed Bel Bachir, who is court chamberlain to the Caliph of Spanish Morocco.

I think we can recruit them, Jack," she was bubbling with excitement. "They are sympathetic to the Free French Forces. They accompanied me to the banquet the Pasha held in my honor, and it was a splendid affair.

The Spanish colonel of the Air Force was there and certain Spanish generals. I was given many presents, and the most valuable: a visa to travel anywhere. Do you understand? I can go anywhere. Back to France even."

She went on, "But it was the same day that the Spanish forcibly occupied the international zone of Tangier. No doubt encouraged to do so by Hitler. Another breach of international law. Maybe this time, I thought, it will finally be enough for America to enter the war ... but they will eventually...I know it." Her features set in that determined expression he knew so well.

"Anyway," she waved her hand expressively, "I was able to survey what happened in the international zone from the comfort and safety of my friend's home in the Spanish Zone.

Bel Bachir did his utmost to help me, and I have here papers from him which are really important concerning the Tangier–German situation. I've never seen an Arab more popular than Bel Bachir. Everywhere he goes, the crowd shouts his name. I think he could be of enormous influence in persuading the Arabs to commit to the cause of the Free French Forces.

Two days later, I reached Lisbon, and there I was able to give our contact the information sent by Paillole and also all the intelligence I had been able to learn in Tangier and Telouet.

Then we put our heads together to try and find a way to get you to Portugal. I approached all my diplomatic contacts in Portugal without success.

Then I organized a couple of performances in Lisbon to demonstrate that I had a reason for going there. After that, I got to thinking that it would be safe enough for you to arrive on one of the coasts of Portugal – I can't bear to be separated from you."

"And look—" She smiled triumphantly as she reached into her handbag and with a twist of her wrist, tossed her hand across the table. An array of sparkling stones rolled across the polished oak surface clattering like dice. Diamonds, rubies, sapphires and emeralds. "A gift from the Pasha."

Angered, unable to curb the jealous beast in his soul, he grabbed her wrist and held it tightly. "And why did he give you those?"

"For the cause," she answered, shaking her wrist from his grip. "Don't worry, I only have eyes for you." She met his gaze as she spoke. Her whole demeanor was convincing. Jack felt reassured, but although he tried to sound genuine when he congratulated her, his voice betrayed his anxiety. In the depths of his consciousness, he could not prevent himself from wondering if the Pasha, who was rumored to have over a hundred women in his harem, also wanted Josephine for himself. He only had to look at her for the answer. What man wouldn't want her? Sadness swamped him in the very moment of Josephine's triumph as he realized that no matter how much she said she loved him and despite their fragile plans for a future together once the war ended, he could never hope to compete with one of the richest men in the world.

Josephine stood up.

"I understand you are anxious about your visa, but I've come back with such good news. I insist we celebrate, then you tell me everything that's happened here while I've been away." She rang for champagne and Jack nodded.

"Yes, of course. I apologize. It's just so infuriating being stuck here."

She held onto his hands. "We have to continue the fight as best we can. You cannot imagine how much it sickened me seeing the Spanish armies install themselves in the

international zone. I prayed that it would be enough to make America act, but still no. I believe the Arabs will join us. The Pasha, Menebhi and Bel Bachir have offered to come here to Casablanca to meet you and to discuss how they can help us. What you are doing is vitally important even though you're stranded here. I can stay here a few days, and then I'll go to Marrakesh to recuperate. I've been offered accommodation there. It'll be more private than this hotel."

Chapter 36

TANGIER, SPRING 1941

Gentle waves rocked the boat. The lapping sound against the bow amplified in the quiet. Josephine stood at the bow unable to resist the call of the approaching city. The ramparted walls rose high above the shore, guarding the inhabitants as they had done for hundreds of years. Soon the sound of the city would drown out the lapping waves and even the sound of the boat's motor as they neared port. Arriving was always so romantic, crossing water to be with a lover. It felt as if she were crossing from one world to another. Behind her the war, ahead a mysterious world where there were no worries or responsibilities, only the moment and the pleasures it brought.

There were yells in Arabic, French, even Spanish. A crowd gathered, having heard perhaps a whisper of her arrival. She sniffed the air. She knew she had arrived in Tangier when she smelt the cinnamon and lemon which hung in the air as tangibly as the scent of honeysuckle in the evening. Here, she was an Arabian princess returning to her lover from whom she had been separated for too long. She had dressed for the part and was wearing her favorite kaftan. The vibrant hues of blue and green elaborately embroidered with gold thread draped elegantly around her body, the silks so fine their touch fell upon her skin like kisses. She pulled the hood over her head as she watched the landing routine. A crewman threw a rope to the porter who secured it to the bollard on the pier. A boarding plank was laid down by the porter who was so intent on looking at her he nearly lost his footing. Josephine stepped onto the pier, her elegant jeweled sandals catching the evening sun. Her maid followed behind, and the porters assigned to carry her luggage scrambled on board, and then followed her, carrying her trunks on their

heads. She walked to the hotel situated on the edge of the pier. Tonight, she would dine alone on her balcony while watching the sea in the moonlight, but first she would go to the Turkish baths with her maid and wash the sand from her body. In the hot steam, she would forget the war, all her worries and pain.

She woke slowly as her maid twittered that the cars had already arrived. She stretched out on the fine linen sheets savoring their cleanliness. After the desert and the sand, every moment had to be enjoyed and treasured.

Dressing – and being dressed – as fast as possible, she and her maid went downstairs, and after checking out of the hotel, Josephine climbed into the first Rolls Royce, her luggage filling the second. As the car rolled slowly along the narrow streets, she experienced the explosion of color and sound that was part of every visit to Tangier. Here a person's color did not even seem noteworthy, the international zone it truly was. Cosmopolitan. Vibrant. Here it was easy to drift back in time and place to the tales of one thousand Arabian nights: snake charmers on street corners, beautiful girls cloaked in mystery, the screeches of monkeys and the cries of begging children with eyes larger than their faces. Everywhere teeming with life, energy, intrigue, mystery, spies. Tangier's position as a city in an international zone was not without its dangers. She shuddered as saw Nazi banners hanging from the windows of some of the private residences.

She leaned back in the leather seats. Outside, the city disappeared giving way to dusty roads and desert. Then the Palace came into view and she could feel her heart beating faster as the car drove up the entrance. The gates swung open as if by some magical force and the cars rolled up the driveway lined with trees flanked by gardens stolen from the desert by complex irrigation systems, the masterpiece of which was a fountain situated in the center of a rectangular lake.

As the vehicle glided to a stop, Bel Bachir came down the steps and opened the door of the Rolls. As she stepped out, he bent kissing her hand.

"It has been too long." He said graciously.

Josephine nodded. "Yes, too long."

They walked up the steps together arm in arm chatting like old friends. Meanwhile, the servants busied themselves unloading her luggage.

As they wandered through the ornate palace gardens, Bel Bachir said, "I wish I could persuade you to stay."

Josephine chuckled. "I wish you could persuade me to stay too." Her eyes sparkled mischievously, and he laughed. "It is the will of Allah." And then he added more thoughtfully, "Allah is wise. It would be too much. I think you would cause havoc. I cannot allow the women here the liberties which you enjoy." He bent, kissing her hand. "I savor your visits as a gift from Allah. It does not become me to seek more than the great Allah chooses to give."

Josephine touched his arm. "I cannot thank you enough for your kindness."

"It is I that am honored to be of assistance."

Josephine dipped into her handbag and produced four passports. "I have these for you." He glanced at them briefly before slipping them into his robe. He then produced a further three passports. "Here are the ones you are waiting for. This family are now Moroccan Jews. They are under the protection of the King. They are free to stay in Morocco where they will be safe, or they can be granted exit visas if they wish."

"Thank you," Josephine said, taking the passports and putting them into her bag. "I will be able to distribute them tomorrow. That is another family you have saved."

Bel Bachir bowed. "I think it is you that has saved them. Now go, before I change my mind and decide to have you thrown into my harem."

Josephine laughed.

"Be careful little one. Everywhere there are spies and traitors. Tangier is like you, beautiful and dangerous." He bent and kissed her hand. "Now I must leave you. I have business which requires my attention. I hope you will honor me with another visit soon."

Chapter 37

CASABLANCA

Jack stared out over the waves watching the boats. Surely one could take him to England. Casablanca felt more like a prison with each day that passed. It was unbearable for a man of action determined to fight for his country to be stranded indefinitely.

The inactivity was as debilitating as a disease. It seemed as if a poison was slowly creeping through his veins and would eventually either kill him or render him completely useless. He gathered what information he could, but the intelligence he gained and was able to transmit to his contact was not of sufficient value to justify his continued presence in Casablanca. Not in his view anyway. He was ready to risk all to make the journey to England, but he was a soldier and his strict orders were to wait. And so, he waited. And waited.

Finally, a message:

"Impossible for you to leave by sea, too complicated. I am unable to forward any more money, even if you send more information."

His reply:

.   .   .

"Sir, May I remind you that I am Captain Jacques Abtey of the Free French Forces. I am neither a spy nor a traitor. I object to being treated by you as a mercenary. I simply wish to take up my position as agreed and to fight for the Free French Forces. Please pass my sentiments to those in command."

Jack waited and waited, one day, two days, a week, a month.

The fisherman, the courier for his messages, came and left twice without further instructions. Despairing of finding a way to join the General in England, Jack decided to join Josephine in Marrakesh.

Chapter 38

MARRAKESH, APRIL 1941

Jack studied the map which Josephine had sent. Already he was deep within the labyrinth that was the Old City. As he penetrated further into the medina, he became conscious with each step that he was leaving behind the civilized face that Marrakesh presented to her tourists and entering the land of one thousand and one nights.

A land which had no place for European customs and sensibilities, a land with rules and traditions which he could never hope to fully understand.

Finally, after following a narrow alleyway, he found himself before an impressive ancient oak door. He knocked three times as he had been instructed. As the door swung open, he found himself staring into the startling blue eyes of a doorkeeper dressed in a long, white robe and with a flowing white beard. A man with so many wrinkles they suggested he was as old as the door he guarded – if not as time itself.

The servant bowed and muttered a greeting in Arabic. He gestured for Jack to follow him. Jack was led first through a mosaic hallway and then through an ornate arched doorway into a courtyard garden where the doorkeeper signaled he should sit.

Jack sat down on the edge of the fountain which took central place in the paved garden. He was impressed immediately with the peacefulness of the setting, a thousand miles away from the bustle of the medina.

Six marbled columns stood around the edges of the courtyard and four orange trees bore fruit. The burbling as the fountain played was a soothing interruption to the silence of the setting. He was filled with a sense of peace.

Josephine appeared as if by magic, dressed in a flowing djellaba. Even with the white cloth of the haik covering her distinctive hair style with only her remarkable eyes visible, there was no mistaking her. He picked her up and swung her round glad to feel her shapeliness beneath the robes. "Isn't it wonderful here," she said. "I've been so happy. Despite missing you terribly," she quickly added having noticed his peeved expression.

"Look at the contentment of the doorman. He has nothing, yet he feels no need of materialistic possessions to find happiness. I've gained a sense of peace while I've been here. I feel transformed. You'll understand. I shall prepare tea for you." She took his hand and led him to a bedroom with doors which opened onto the courtyard. "First dress. Here are some robes that I got for you." Lying on the bed were a djellaba and traditional sandals. "Get ready and join me."

Jack put on the clothes. He had always resisted the temptation to "go native" and had never worn traditional dress before. The robes were obviously of quality, and he found their looseness strangely liberating. When he returned to the courtyard, Josephine was already setting the glasses for tea on the ornate wooden table, which appeared to be placed by the sides of the low sofas for that very purpose.

Her movements were elegant and flowing as she crushed the mint leaves in her hands before allowing the fragments to fall into the teapot. He watched mesmerized. It appeared as if Josephine had thrown her wildness aside and adopted an Eastern approach to life. He knew in his heart that could never be possible. She had no idea how to be a subservient woman, and there was no curbing her temper. Yet the illusion was intoxicating to witness.

She bowed to him as she gestured silently for him to take his place on the couch. Jack felt a moment of anxiety. Much as he bemoaned Josephine's temper, he would not change her. The image of her as a woman devoid of opinions was not a comforting one.

SOME WEEKS LATER

"Listen to the bird singing, to the water of the fountain, to the silence." She lay on the lounger, body motionless, eyes fixed on the sky, absorbed completely by the beauty of nature and the tranquility of their surroundings.

"They say that Africa crushes all by her embrace. That the bravest and strongest of men, if they try to confront her, die stupidly, atrociously. It's true, Jack, isn't it? I've found such peace here by adopting the local way of life. Our friends have shown us the wonders of their civilization – from the ancient palaces – built centuries ago – to the tribes in the remote mountains who live in houses extended from caves. We've learned so much of their history. We've been welcomed into the tents of Nomads, Bedouin, Teuchars and Berbers, the tribes who have lived in and traversed the Sahara for centuries. I've danced the 'Guedra' with the indigo clad Teuchar women."

Jack nodded. It was true. They had learned to respect and admire the culture of the people of North Africa, their attitude to life, their generosity and hospitality. In their private courtyard, it was too easy to forget the war.

Josephine laughed, disappeared for a few minutes and then returned wearing a traditional dancing costume. In the background, Jack could hear the sounds of the prayers from the Mosque Ben Youssef, "lā ilāha illā allāh," but the sound drifted from his consciousness as Josephine commanded his complete attention.

Mesmerized, he watched her very individual interpretation of the "Shikhat," the belly dance.

She twirled before him shaking her hips. Her hands stretched out as she twirled around, holding a scarlet red scarf across her hips to emphasize her gyrations. Her jeweled belt rattled like a musical instrument such was the speed of her movements. Here, she was his and his alone. If only...

Chapter 39

MARRAKESH, MAY 1941

"We can't hide from the war any longer, Jack. Let's go to Spain. I can arrange some performances."

Jack laughed. "Have you forgotten that Spain is sympathetic to Hitler and all he stands for? Don't forget that they have some splendid prisons there, or perhaps you would prefer to experience the dungeons. Do you think your smile will make them forget you're black? I've no doubt that even a short period as a guest would have a cooling effect on that spirit of yours."

"I refuse to do nothing."

"You forget we're in the army. Our orders are to wait."

"Wait, wait. That's all we do. Well, I can't wait. Not any longer!"

"Go on then. Don't listen to me. Don't pay the slightest attention to anyone else. I hope when you're captured it is not the instruments of the Spanish Inquisition that they use to torture you." Jack turned away from her and watched the monkeys jumping from one orange tree to another. Here it was too easy to forget about the war. He felt a blinding pain in his shoulder as Josephine attacked him screaming.

"You coward! So that is what you have in your heart. Water, thin and rancid from a poisoned well. Not the blood of a man. The blood of a patriot." Eyes blazing and hair wild like a banshee, she started pummeling his chest with her fists. "Come on, Jack, you dirty coward."

Jack seized her wrists, gripping them tightly as she struggled to free herself.

"Listen to me," he said staring intently into her eyes. "I just want you to realize how dangerous it is."

Enraged, she continued her tirade. "Do I look like an idiot?"

Jack did not answer. She was giving a very good impersonation of a crazed person.

"After living here, accepting the hospitality of our friends here, do you think I would desert them? Look, I have it all mapped out."

"Calm down, I won't release you until you promise to behave. I will listen."

They stared angrily at each other until finally she nodded.

Jack let go, and she sat down meekly, producing from her chair a sheet of paper scrawled with writing. "Here," she said in her most persuasive voice, "is my program, check it over. What do you take me for? An innocent, a peasant from the countryside, a dove from the skies? I am ready. Will you come with me? I know what I'm doing. I hope I shall be brave enough to pull it off. But you, do you have the courage to come with me?"

Jack replied angrily, "You know I don't have the papers to travel. I'm stuck here. But I won't do nothing. I'll go back to Casablanca and try to make fresh contact with the British. You go if you must." He grabbed her arms before continuing with tenderness in his voice, "But be careful. Promise me."

Chapter 40

CASABLANCA, MID JUNE 1941

Jack passed Josephine a glass of champagne. "Well done," he said as their glasses clinked. He leafed through the notes she had brought back from Tetouan, Seville, Madrid and Barcelona. Intelligence gained from careless talk in foreign embassies and from her own eyes as she travelled from country to country. "I hardly feel like celebrating," she replied somberly. "Why to arrive here, you would think the Nazis had already won the war. I saw Nazi officers parading through the streets as I arrived and Nazi flags flying from domains in the Sousse."

He smiled. "I have some intelligence of my own."

Curious, she responded, "Oh really?"

He paused, savoring the moment. "Yes. After you left, I managed to make contact with Canfield. He's the American vice-consul in Casablanca. Just been posted here"

"That's great."

Jack paused again. It was not often he trumped Josephine in the intelligence game.

"And?" She looked at him more intently this time. Then she went over to him. "And what?"

Jack laughed , picked her up and twirled her round. "And he has been sent here to oversee the merchandise sent to North Africa in preparation for possible landings should America decide to join the war. In that event, it is envisaged American troops will join the British and Free French." Josephine screeched with pleasure and hugged him. "He wants to meet our Moroccan friends. And he wants me to stay in Casablanca for the moment. He says I'll be invaluable here to help with the preparations for the landings when the time comes. I've agreed, subject to permission from London."

Chapter 41

PLACE DEJEMAA EL FNA
MARRAKESH, JUNE 1941

The snake charmer's flute was almost drowned by the hammering of drums, the clatter of 'qraqab' or metal castanets and the strains of the 'ghaita' heralding the arrival of a 'Gnaoua' troupe of dancers who cartwheeled into the square in a kaleidoscope of color.

Josephine watched fascinated by the movements of the dance traditionally invoked to drive away evil spirits. Then her attention was drawn to a poor soul who was having his tooth extracted by the street dentist with a dubious set of pliers.

The square never failed to captivate her. From the entertainers to the spice traders, from the magicians to the potion sellers wandering through the market, it was like entering an enchanted kingdom.

As she began to move towards the street of slipper stalls, her eyes fixed on a man moving towards her with purpose. He was completely bald and dressed in a white jibba. He seemed familiar, but yet she did not recognize him. Suddenly, she screamed as realization dawned. "Jack!" She burst into riotous laughter. Passers-by, curious at her outburst, stopped to watch.

"Jack," she said touching his head as he finally reached her. "I didn't recognize you."

"Do you like it?"

"Why ... I have never in my life seen such a perfectly shaped head. You must take a photo and send it to the Natural History Museum so they can preserve it for the benefit of humanity. If you were trying to make yourself unrecognizable, you've succeeded." Her taunting attracted the attention of the bread-sellers, the women, usually so

subservient, at their stalls began to point at Jack, their eyes, the only part of their face visible, sparkled. Their hilarity spread to the shy women who managed the jewelry stalls. Jack soon became the focus of laughter in the medina square.

"Jack," Josephine shrieked between peals of laughter. "You're becoming the main attraction in this square of miracles."

Entering the spirit of frivolity, Jack bowed as if he had just completed a performance. Some of the stall holders clapped. Then Josephine took his hand. "Come on, let's go home." She became more serious as they came to the walled edge of the square. Crouched on the ground were old people holding out in their withered hands bowls for coins. A string of blind people walked past, led by a child dressed in rags. They held hands, one ghost leading the other, six bodies virtually devoid of life, chanting in sad monotonous voices, "Look at our eyes, our eyes without sight, take pity on us because our suffering is eternal. Allah is great. Allah will reward you."

"How is it possible, my darling, not to help such suffering," Josephine said to Jack emptying her purse into the hands of the unfortunates.

When they reached their home, they found that Bayonne had arrived, and Josephine's good humor returned as Jack explained the benefits of a double zero haircut. They spent an enjoyable evening listening to each other's adventures, but a few hours later that night Josephine experienced severe stomach cramps. The pain intensified, and the first thing the next morning, Jack called the doctor.

Coming out of her bedroom, the doctor looked very serious. Jack felt his heart sink.

"Josephine has always enjoyed good health, and she's never suffered intestinal problems," he explained.

"I don't think the problem is to do with her intestines, but I have no idea what is wrong with her. For the moment, there's nothing more I can tell you. I shall return tomorrow

morning. Send for some ice, break it into little pieces and wrap it in cloth, then apply the compress where she is most fevered and in pain. You must bring her temperature down if she is to have any hope of recovery."

Bayonne left with the doctor to fetch ice, and Jack went to Josephine's room. She was lying on the bed, grasping her stomach, her face ashen.

"Mon Dieu! Josephine, what's wrong?" He took her hand. It was burning hot.

Delirious, she murmured, "Jack, what's wrong? I'm struggling even to breathe."

"It's nothing serious," he said, as he stroked her brow. "Bayonne will be back shortly with some ice, and we'll make a compress. Then you'll feel better."

About thirty minutes later, Bayonne returned with the ice, which was applied as instructed, but it did little to ease her pain or lessen the fever.

The doctor's words had devastated Jack and he could feel himself falling apart. It seemed the only solution was to get Josephine to Casablanca and into a hospital.

As there was no transport suitable for taking the patient there, he left by train intending to commission an ambulance from Casablanca.

The train journey was unending. It was the first time he was not charmed by the passengers on the roof and the melee of life that seemed to form part of any train journey in Morocco.

Frantic with worry, he arrived at the hospital and demanded an ambulance immediately. The clerk shook his head. "I am sorry, sir, we have no vehicles here capable of making the journey to Marrakesh. It is five hundred kilometers over tracks, not proper roads."

Desolate, Jack sat on the steps of the hospital. Josephine needed him. He would not fail her. He remembered the Stanleys and their reliable, albeit battered, station wagon. It could be adapted to carry a patient and was capable of making the journey. He set off running for their house.

After driving all night, Jack parked the car as close as he could to the medina. When he arrived, Bayonne shook his head. Jack rushed into Josephine's room. She lay listless on the bed, still in the grip of the terrible fever. Bayonne joined him. "I think it would be better if we wait until night. At least it will be cooler."

Jack breathed deeply, his heart pounding, mind racing. Every second could be vital, but the sailor was right. Trying to cross the desert in the daytime could prove more dangerous than waiting. He glanced at his watch and nodded. "We can get the car ready, and then leave at eight."

Five hours later, Jack and Bayonne summoned the servants. Two men gripped the poles at the front and Jack and Bayonne those behind. The four of them carried Josephine on the makeshift stretcher out of the house. It was a nightmare. The narrow alleys of the medina seemed to have become even narrower, the steps even steeper, the pathways more uneven. Every time they knocked a corner of the stretcher against one of the walls, Josephine moaned and Jack winced.

Eventually, she was secured as comfortably as possible in the car, dressed warmly because the desert nights were cold. At the pace of a funeral procession, the car rolled out of Marrakesh. Above, the stars were spread across the sky, like a beautiful map to guide them to their destination, but Jack's eyes were fixed on the track before them, trying to avoid every bump and dip that could cause discomfort to his passenger. Josephine was not even conscious of her surroundings. It was a long journey.

The morning sun had already driven the cold of night away when they arrived at the hospital where a room had been reserved. Jack pulled the car to a stop directly outside the steps leading to the entrance. A nurse wearing a Red Cross insignia came down the steps to greet them. Jack shouted, "I need help to carry the stretcher."

The woman shook her head. "There is no one available. She will need to climb the steps herself."

"Look at her," he retorted pointing at Josephine who was obviously delirious. "She can't walk."

"There are only twelve steps."

"I've driven all night to get here."

The nurse shrugged. "What can I do? There is no one here who can help."

Shaking his head, Jack leapt back into the car and slammed the door of the vehicle shut. With a roar of engine and screech of tires, the car accelerated. The frightened nurse leapt backwards to the safety of the steps.

Jack spotted a policeman. He stopped and asked for directions to a decent hospital. Shortly afterwards, he parked the station wagon outside the Mers Sultan Clinic. Jack breathed a sigh of relief. The hospital appeared modern and was built in the style of a pleasant bungalow. White walls covered with bougainvillea were flooded with sunlight. A meticulously dressed woman with a kind smile arrived to greet them, and Josephine was soon installed in a clean bright room. It felt like a place where it would be possible to recover. It was evident from the expressions of the medics that Josephine would not be able to leave for some time. Jack requested a camp bed so he could sleep in her room, and the staff made the arrangements rapidly without question. He could not bear to leave her.

Chapter 42

CASABLANCA, JUNE 1941

Jack and the doctor stood outside Josephine's room.

"Is she awake now?"

Jack nodded.

"I must tell her, then."

"No, let me do it. Please. I think it's best."

"Very well. I'll leave it to your judgement. In any case, I'll call to see her later." Before leaving, the doctor touched his arm. "I'm sorry. There was nothing that could be done."

Jack watched the doctor walk away from him down the corridor. His footsteps were the only sound to be heard in the calm sterile serenity of the hospital. It was all so at odds with the churning sickness in his stomach. He was sure that this was going to be the hardest thing he would ever have to do. Taking a deep breath, he turned the doorknob and entered.

The overpowering smell of lilies swamped the smell of disinfectant that pervaded everywhere else in the hospital. Bouquets of flowers filled the bedside table and lined the walls in a selection of vases. Josephine had sat up, and although still drowsy from the anesthetic, she looked bright. Despite her weakened state, the flowers paled beside her.

Jack pulled his camp bed closer to her bed. He took her hands in his and noticed how thin they felt. He looked straight into her eyes and said, "I'm so sorry, Josephine. The doctor was here, but I wanted to tell you myself."

"The baby," she whispered.

He shook his head slowly. "I'm sorry."

Her head dipped. Her hands tensed, gripping his so hard her fingernails bit into his flesh.

"We can try again, Josephine."

Her eyes searched his. Her hands tugged as she tried to pull them from his . He gripped them. "Look at me. All I care about is you. That you are here. I mean it, Josephine." He could see her blink back tears and try to summon her strength, try to hide how devastated she was. No matter how bravely she appeared to accept the loss, he knew in his heart this was catastrophic news. She'd been so excited to discover she'd become pregnant. Fear gripped his heart as he remembered her words at Milandes about her ex-husband. She'd told him that losing Jean's child had finished their relationship. He would not let that happen to them. The war had robbed them of too much already.

Chapter 43

CASABLANCA, SEPTEMBER 1941

Jack looked at her lying still on the bed. It was heart-breaking for him to see her so lifeless. They had bound their fates together for as long as they were partners in espionage, for the duration of the war. Now they were going to begin another war, a fight that he was determined to win. The enemy was different, but he was no less committed. They would win the battle for Josephine's life. They had to. He felt like they were soulmates bound together for eternity.

Days passed. Jack slept by Josephine's bed, there to respond to her every need, to wet her lips if she was thirsty, to hold her hand if she cried out in the night, to place a compress on her forehead when the fever returned, to make sure that she was never alone.

The doctor had been brutally honest when he gave his prognosis. She was strong. She might recover, but her chances were one in a thousand.

It was there in the hospital, holding her fevered hand, not in the field of battle, that Jack learned what it is to be human and what is important in life. To be rich or poor, famous or unknown, is of no consequence when one is fighting death.

Chapter 44

CASABLANCA, CHRISTMAS 1941

Jack peeped round the door. Josephine seemed to be dozing, so he crept into the room. If he was careful, he could surprise her as planned. He assembled the miniature tree and began decorating it carefully with the paper silhouettes, which he cut out with scissors he had borrowed from a nurse. Red and green paper he had avidly collected. Silver balls made from scrunched up chocolate wrappers. When he was finished, the tree looked quite impressive, considering. He leaned back to appreciate his work. Then he placed a wrapped package under the tree. It was Christmas and they would celebrate, although it would be a far cry from that lavish first Christmas they'd spent together at Vesinet.

Clap, clap.

He turned to see Josephine sitting up in bed. She looked pale and thin, but her face was glowing. "It looks wonderful," she exclaimed, sounding better than she had for weeks.

He smiled and leaned over to lightly kiss her. "I thought you were sleeping."

"I was, but when I woke up and saw what a wonderful job you were making of the tree, I couldn't bear to disturb you."

"It's not bad," he said, laughing, then more seriously, he added, "I hope it's our last one here. The last one of the war."

"I'll drink to that. Do we have some champagne?"

Jack dipped into his bag and produced a bottle with a flourish. "Of course, mademoiselle, it *is* Christmas after all."

Josephine giggled with excitement as he held out a glass.

"To Christmases," she said. Jack sat beside her on the bed, holding her hand tenderly.

"Remember that first Christmas we spent together?" She squeezed his hand.

Jack smiled at the memory. "I'll never forget that night. I couldn't believe it when I arrived. There you were in the lounge in front of a blazing fire surrounded by what must have been hundreds of children's presents. I thought for a moment that the world had gone mad. I thought you were unwrapping the presents, and I wondered who could have sent you such an odd assortment of things."

Josephine laughed. "In those days, my suitors sent me diamonds and rubies, not books and dolls."

"It was the best Christmas ever, though."

She nodded. "Yes, little did you realize when you accepted my invitation that you would be transforming into Father Jack Christmas."

"I'll never forget the looks on those children's faces when we delivered their presents. It was something, wasn't it? We'll do it again. When the war is over."

A shadow crossed over her face, and Jack felt a cold shiver down his spine. Her features were suddenly blank as though she did not see him.

"We can and we will, Josephine. When the war's over, we can still have a life, children, everything you want."

She pulled her hand from his. "The living is now," she replied looking resolutely at the tree. Jack sighed, thinking of the number of times they said, "When the war is over."

All their plans seemed to hinge on when the war would be over. In his blackest moments, he wondered if it would ever end. He had almost lost hope during the nights when Josephine seemed to be slipping away, when the fever gripped so tightly it seemed she could never recover.

But now he feared that the war was going to rob them of their future even if they both made it to the end.

She had not spoken about their plans for after the war since she'd lost the baby and a new fear had entered his heart. What if she just wanted him out of her future because he reminded her of her loss, her failure, as she seemed to view it. She'd told him she couldn't bear the sight of her husband after she had miscarried their child and that was the ultimate source of their separation. Jack worried that he might suffer the same fate. Was the possibility of the war never ending better than losing the war? Even if they won the war, would he lose her? Their fates were bound together until then at least. What could he do other than make her see that he was there for her, no matter what?

So, Jack put his own fears aside. All that really mattered was that she recover. He admired her spirit so much. She never seemed to consider that they might lose the war. America had now entered it, but perhaps it was too late. France had already lost it. He and Josephine might be fighting under the flag of the Free French Forces and General de Gaulle, but they were doing so in secrecy. He wondered how long the situation could continue. Overwhelmed with emotion, he took Josephine's hands in his, wishing with all his heart he could make her well. She was so thin now, reduced to a shadow of herself by the war and all it represented.

Chapter 45

CASABLANCA 1942

Jack could see by the doctor's expression it was bad news.

"Would you like to come to my office?" he asked.

Jack shook his head. He didn't need to walk down the corridor to know what was coming.

"Perhaps you should sit down," the doctor gestured to the chair positioned outside Josephine's room. "There has been no improvement. She's so weak now it will be virtually impossible to shake off the infection. I'm sorry. You should prepare for the worst."

The words, although expected, hit him like a bullet. Outside the sun blazed, yet in this stark corridor, the light was being stolen from his world. She was impossible to live with – but to live without her was beyond contemplation.

"I want to stay with her."

The doctor nodded. "Of course. Does she have any requests?"

Jack looked at him, puzzled.

"A priest? A rabbi? Her admission form is ambiguous as regards her religion."

"Oh, yes. She is a believer in all religions," Jack explained. "I know she would want someone. A priest, I think." He was struggling to come to terms with the doctor's diagnosis.

"I will arrange for that." The doctor placed his hand on Jack's arm. "I know it's hard. She's so young." They both stood looking at Josephine. She lay peacefully on the bed in a deep sleep. Despite the gauntness of her features, she looked serenely beautiful. In the silence, it was just possible to hear her faint breathing.

The priest arrived almost immediately, and Jack wondered if he'd been summoned even before the doctor had approached him. After the briefest of introductions, he set about the rituals of his office. The familiar Latin incantation of the last rites in the priest's melodious voice was so at odds with the clamor of the city outside with all its foreignness. After everything she'd been through, it didn't seem possible to Jack that she'd been destined to die in this strange country alone, except for himself, far from her beloved France. He could feel tears welling in his eyes and he was not ashamed to shed them. The priest folded the rosary beads and placed them in their box. He lifted his bible and returned it to his bag. He put on his hat. "Do you wish to discuss the funeral arrangements?"

Jack shook his head vehemently. The priest nodded, aware he had gone too far. "If you would like me to come back, just let the hospital know."

Josephine had remained motionless throughout the ceremony. How unlike her, he thought wistfully. Such energy, such passion, she was barely recognizable as the same person when she was still.

Chapter 46

ST LOUIS 1942

Margaret rushed into the house waving the paper. Tears flowed down her cheeks as she sobbed, "Mama, look."

Carrie McDonald made a dismissive sound as she took the paper from her daughter's hands and read the headline: JOSEPHINE BAKER DIES.

"Tumpy ain't dead," she said, and went back to stirring the soup.

Chapter 47

CASABLANCA, 8 NOVEMBER 1942

Jack leaned forward picking up the leaflet that had fluttered through the window. He passed it to Josephine. "Well, Looks like the landings are about to begin." He took Josephine's hand. "I think you should leave here. In case there's shelling."

"No," she said firmly. "I'm staying here. It's the safest place for me. Anyway, you heard de Gaulle's instructions to the French. Do Not Resist. And what would the staff think? It will arouse suspicion if I leave. You know I'm watched. And I can't believe the French soldiers stationed here will fight the Allies.

"It's too complicated to predict. What do you think?" Jack turned to ask the British Ambassador who was visiting.

"I understand that Giraud will broadcast from Morocco tonight to request that the French welcome the Allies to their shores. Allied troops will be told to accept any French surrender. It's been emphasized to the Allied Forces that they must understand that the French units are not Germans or Japanese," he continued. "If you're insistent on staying here, look for flashlight beams shining vertically in the air. That's the signal by which the French troops can indicate their surrender."

"I pray there'll be no resistance. It breaks my heart to think about what happened to the sailors of the *Britannia*."

Everyone looked worried, but then Josephine suddenly brightened. "Look, we should be celebrating. How long have we waited for this? Tomorrow we will be another step closer to a free France. We should have some champagne; don't you think? I have a bottle hidden away for this very occasion. Maria, some glasses, please."

They toasted, clinking glasses. "To the landing."

"I should be out there," Jack muttered.

"You can't go. Remember, you're wanted for desertion. If you're recognized as Jacques Abtey, you could be shot on the spot."

He laughed. "But I'm Jacques Herbert now." He raised his spectacles and wiggled his eyebrows up and down. "I promise I'm not leaving you. Not tonight of all nights. We'll face whatever happens together."

"Do we have any further indications of what the attitude of Vichy French Forces will be?" asked the Ambassador.

"I've been having discreet conversations with the secretary, but the situation is complex. The Vichy Government want the landings to be successful, but they can't risk compromising the position of their neutral status in mainland France. For the Vichy soldiers positioned here, there's always been the covert threat of reprisals to family back home if there's any evidence of a breach of France's surrender treaty with Germany. The French units here dare not take responsibility for causing the German invasion of the rest of mainland France as a result of their colluding with Allied Forces landing in French Territories. The only way of proving they haven't colluded is to fight."

"Mon Dieu," muttered Josephine. "To think we have come to this, tomorrow French men may fight French men on the streets of Casablanca."

Chapter 48

CASABLANCA, 9 NOVEMBER 1942

In the small hours, the sound of shelling shattered the silence.

"It's started," Josephine whispered, alarm all too apparent on her face. "Look for the signal." Jack pulled back the curtain. Turning, he shook his head. "It seems the worst has come to the worst," he said sadly as he stepped out onto the terrace searching skyward for the beams which would signal surrender.

"Help me," she said, struggling to get out of bed. Jack supported her as she walked to the terrace in her pajamas and an old knitted top. Holding hands, they watched as flash after flash lit up the night sky as vivid as a lightning storm. Each moment of blinding light accompanied by a thunderous crash of sound like an unaccomplished orchestra playing to a hellish firework display. Josephine flinched with each shell, as she leaned against him feebly for support. "There," she said with surprising strength in her voice. "I told you the Americans would come."

The sky began to glow a smoky red as shells struck buildings and fires took hold across the city. Jack wondered anxiously if he should have insisted on moving her to a safer location.

Chapter 49

CASABLANCA 10 NOVEMBER 1942

The hours passed. They watched and waited, able only to guess what dawn would bring. Morning came and still the rattle of machine guns competed with the thump of artillery. News came in trickles. The Americans had landed. The French admiral charged with the defense of Casablanca was determined to hold the city against the invaders. One day passed and then another. It appeared that the French intended to fight the Allies to the last sailor, to the last Senegalese and until Casablanca was reduced to nothing more than dust.

"I have to do something," Jack said. "I can't stand by and watch this any longer. Why are the French fighting? To keep their word to Hitler, who is turning Europe into a slave state for the Aryan super race? They can't believe that dying here in Casablanca will be enough to stop the Nazis occupying the whole of France."

The ambulance rolled along the street. Jack steered carefully, avoiding the shell craters in the road. Under the Red Cross banner, he and a colleague, Villon, had moved without challenge from the French sector into the American side. The first soldier they saw, obviously dead, was Senegalese. He had died fighting for Hitler, who would have sent him to a death camp. Jack's stomach churned.

Further on, they saw the twisted corpse of an American soldier and then several more from the Senegalese unit.

Jack continued, finally sighting the first American troops lying in a ditch, their rifles pointing in the other direction. Jack called out, "Hello, where is your commanding officer?" A soldier pointed and Jack saw further along a man of not more than twenty-five years old who glanced at them with little interest. After some persuasion, he instructed one of his men to take them to the commander of his regiment. Once there, they were received by a Lieutenant Colonel who communicated their arrival to General Patton. Ten minutes later, they were in a jeep driven by a captain en route to a meeting with General Patton himself. Eventually, they arrived at Fedela, at the entrance to a farm. They were challenged by a sentry who aimed his machine gun at them. The Captain explained their mission briefly to the guard, but then without explanation the jeep did an about turn. "Sorry, guys," their driver explained. "The General considers it of no benefit to receive you at this time."

"But it's vital," Jack insisted.

"I'm sorry, but there's nothing more I can do for you." The Captain returned them to his unit, then with a friendly beep of his horn, left them by the roadside.

"It's a damn nuisance we didn't keep the ambulance," Villon commented wryly. "It's going to be much more difficult to get back through to the French side and we have at least a ten kilometer walk ahead of us."

As the men tramped along the road they were forced to dive into a ditch as an impressive car displaying the French tricolor on a flag on the bonnet swept past at speed. Eventually, a French lorry stopped and took them to the gates of the city. There they learned that the French Forces in Casablanca had attended a meeting and peace had resulted, which explained why their meeting with Patton had been cancelled so abruptly. The avenue by the station was packed with people awaiting the liberation. Jack rushed back to the hospital. When he entered Josephine's bedroom, she was gone. Frantic, he sought out a nurse, who pointed upwards. Jack sped up the stairs to the roof. There she was watching the sky.

"Look, it's happening." He pointed upwards and they watched together as a beam of light pointed skyward. It was followed by another and another until ribbons of light patterned the sky. The shelling and gunfire had stopped completely.

"They've stopped fighting. Praise God. Everything is finally going to plan." She produced another bottle of champagne, and Jack laughed.

"This is the beginning of the end for Germany. This is the first step on the long road back to France." They raised their glasses.

Chapter 50

CASABLANCA, 11 NOVEMBER 1942

Josephine struggled onto the balcony. "There is no way I am going to miss this." Her heart pounded and she could feel strength beginning to seep into her bones. Flags waved and a brass band sounded joyfully, as the procession moved past. Americans with the Stars and Stripes. The Free French with their tricolor with the Cross of Lorraine superimposed. The British with their Union Jack. Finally, the French army with the tricolor. Who would believe that only days before they had been in bitter conflict? How cruel that men had died so needlessly. Her eyes filled with tears of both joy and sadness. What words could describe how she felt? To know that the tide had finally turned here in Casablanca before her very eyes. Everyone knew it was only a matter of time now before the Nazis were defeated. The only real question was how many more lives would be lost in this terrible conflict.

They raised their glasses of champagne to America, to France, to Britain.

Chapter 51

CASABLANCA, LATE
NOVEMBER 1942

Jack shook his head slowly. What else could he do? The soldier before him was too infirm to be accepted into the Free French Army. The man looked crushed.

That was normal. It was tantamount to a death warrant. He had defected from a French post under the command of General Noguès who was still fighting against the Allies. Already his name would be on the list of military deserters which Jack would be given tomorrow by the Vichy police in Casablanca. The rejected soldier would be unable to use his own name or his ration card because he was a deserter. With no ration card, there would be no food.

Jack signaled his aide. "See to it that this man is given a new identity and the necessary ration cards. Next," he called without looking up. "Name?" "Emmanuel Bayonne."

Jack threw down his pen, got up, walked round the desk and hugged his friend. "Take over for a few minutes," Jack instructed his aide. "I think this deserves a drink. How did you get here?"

"When the Nazis invaded Vichy France on the twelfth, I left Milandes. I managed to escape over the Pyrenees, then through Spain to here. What a journey."

"Good man," Jack said. "All hell is breaking loose here. I'm in charge of admissions to the Free French Forces. As you can see, we are flooded with applicants. Refugees from France. Zimmer has arrived here too.

We have to put in place a means to lodge, clothe and feed these men. Then equip and arm them as rapidly as possible. Even men with white hair who're well over fifty have insisted on being accepted.

They've left their wives and children to fight for France. They come with their water flasks and their old muskets ready to fight for liberty. We're accepting them because despite everything, they're not frightened of the Nazis. They are ready to fight for their country to the end."

Chapter 52

CASABLANCA, 1 DECEMBER 1942

As the jeep rolled along the docks, Josephine felt like Rip Van Winkel. It was so long ago she'd been admitted to the hospital, to be finally discharged seemed like a miracle in itself. But Casablanca had been transformed during her convalescence.The noise was phenomenal. Banging and clanking. Constant activity as a relay of boats brought supplies and men ashore from the ships anchored in the harbor. Trains, tanks, jeeps were being constructed before her eyes, with the American logo. GIs roamed the streets, young men in their uniforms staring in wonder at the street entertainers and women draped in kaftans. Occasionally, soldiers waved. She waved back but doubted they recognized her. Wearing shades and with legs like matchsticks, she felt very frail, but she'd been pressuring the doctor for her discharge since the liberation of Casablanca. She had to see what was happening for herself. She was filled with excitement; the whole town was on a wave of hope. You could feel it in the air as tangible as the sand. With America in the war, it was just a matter of time until the Nazis were defeated. After their tour, Jack drove her to the train station. "I'm sorry I can't join you at Menehbi's palace in Marrakesh, but I can't leave here at the moment. Promise me you will rest."

She smiled and nodded. "Of course, I will. I'll see you at Christmas?"

"You bet."

Chapter 53

MARRAKESH, CHRISTMAS 1942

The doorman bowed as Jack approached the palace entrance and led him immediately to Menebhi.

"Haven't you been told? Josephine is at the Hotel Mamounai. She contracted a typhoid virus, so she moved there three days ago."

Jack's heart stopped. Was there no end?

"Do you wish to have tea?" Menebhi offered.

"No," Jack shouted. He was already running towards the door.

When he entered her bedroom, he was shocked by Josephine's appearance. Droplets of sweat formed on her flushed face and she appeared semi-conscious.

"Jack," she gasped, struggling to sit up in bed. "Is it really you?" She then collapsed back onto the pillow. Alarmed, he rushed to her bedside and touched her brow. It was burning hot.

"Thank goodness you're here. I think I've been possessed by a devil. And he is only interested in making me ill."

He smiled at her attempt at humor as he clasped her hand, but anxiety was uppermost.

"My love, why did you not send for me? You know that I would have come at once."

There was an almost imperceptible nod. "I know how important your work is."

"You must promise to send for me if you need me. I will come. Nothing could stop me. Not winter. Not war. Not that damned desert track between here and Casablanca."

She smiled weakly and squeezed his hand. Jack sent the maid for ice and fresh water. "And fetch me some White Horse whisky," he added as she left the room. "We're going to celebrate. It's our tradition." When the maid returned with the items, Jack said, "I'll take over, you can take the evening off."

He sat in the chair by Josephine's bed and wiped her face with the cool water. She sat up and seemed a little better. He poured a generous portion of whisky into his glass and raised it.

"To your good health," he toasted. "May you finish the war with the Nazis once you have finished battling with microbes."

She almost managed a laugh. "How can it be that I'm confined to this damnable bed yet again? I am tired of this battle."

Downstairs, they could hear the strains of jazz music and American soldiers singing, celebrating Christmas.

Jack knocked back a shot of whisky. "This won't do," he said.

"Don't leave ..."

But the door was already closed behind him. In moments, he returned with his contraband. A branch from the tree that stood in the hotel reception area, some oranges, lemons, candles, paper and scissors. He set to work and in no time at all a miniature Christmas tree in all its glory took pride of place by the window of the hotel room.

NEXT DAY

"I'm sorry I have to leave," Jack explained, holding her hands. "I will telephone every day to see how you are. And if you need me, you must send word. I'll come immediately."

"Thank you, Jack."

Chapter 54

MARRAKESH, FEBRUARY 1943

"Madam, a visitor. Sidney Williams, director of The Liberty Club."

Josephine glanced up from the magazine she'd been reading. "Of course, but he needs no introduction."

She gestured to a cushioned bench and sat up, determined he wouldn't see the pain the movement caused. "Please sit down. Some tea...or champagne, perhaps?" she offered with a wink.

"Tea would be most welcome."

Josephine nodded to the maid.

She and the visitor chatted together while waiting for the tea to arrive.

The maid returned promptly with the tea, a tall ornate jug and small glasses. She poured their drinks and then left the room.

The visitor got to the point. "I've come to ask a favor."

"Go on..."

"We have a great many soldiers in Casablanca and Morocco as a whole who need to be entertained. As you know, The Liberty Club was established by the Red Cross, and having the good fortune to have you in our midst, I wondered if we could prevail on you to make an appearance for the troops."

Josephine perked up.

"There is, however, a financial restraint," he added looking uncomfortable. "We have a very limited budget. We couldn't meet the fee your appearance would merit."

"I never ask payment for entertaining troops, but I do have some conditions which must be met."

"Of course." Mr. Williams made no effort to hide his delight. To think that Josephine Baker had agreed to perform at an establishment under his control was an honor beyond imagining.

"My gratis performances are for the armed forces only, no civilian personnel."

"That is quite acceptable." Mr. Williams nodded. "Now, if we can arrange a suitable date."

"Oh, but I haven't finished," Josephine continued, shaking her finger as if he were a naughty child. "I'm only prepared to perform if the audience is not segregated."

His expression shifted immediately and noticeably from the ecstatic to the stunned.

"But Miss Baker, you understand that the club operates on a segregated basis. The time is apportioned equally between the white and black clientele. I assure you that there is a strict anti-racism policy in operation."

"My terms are non-negotiable," she said smiling graciously. "We've got to show that blacks and whites are treated equally in the American Army or else what's the point in waging war on Hitler."

"Well ... of course, Miss Baker ... I understand completely. It's just ... never been done before. You do understand my difficulty ..."

"Nonsense, Mr. Williams. The American Army might choose to divide its men into different units by their color, but I refuse to divide my audience, not by race, not by religion, not by color." She held up her arm. "White or black, Mr. Williams. Where would you put a coffee-colored Negress?"

He flushed with embarrassment. "Miss Baker ..." He stood up and gave a neat bow. "We will be honored at The Liberty Club to have you perform. I see no reason why we can't meet with your conditions." He pulled out his diary and asked, "When is suitable?"

"The sooner the better. We don't want to keep the boys waiting. There's a war on you know."

A LITTLE LATER

"How could you?" Jack shouted.

"Calm down."

"I'm coming straight back with the doctor," he raged, and stormed out of the room.

Josephine struggled to sit up and demanded the maid bring her a mirror. She studied her reflection. She was barely recognizable – her face was so thin and grey. "My makeup," she called.

By the time Jack returned with the doctor, she was sitting up, made up and bejeweled.

"You can't fool the doctor," Jack muttered.

The doctor shook his head. "Really, Josephine, you know very well you've unhealed surgical scars on your stomach. You must rest until you've completely healed. Any strain or vigorous actively could jeopardize your recuperation and even your life. I forbid it."

Josephine thumped her fist on the table. "Don't you realize how important this is. The Liberty Club has agreed to a non-segregated audience. Blacks and whites together. It is the first step towards ending prejudice against colored people. I won't miss this opportunity." The doctor and Jack looked at each other in silence.

She adopted a gentler, more persuasive, tone. "I'll be careful. I promise."

The two men stared at her shaking their heads. She folded her arms defiantly.

"You promise to go easy," Jack said finally.

The doctor said curtly, "My advice, in the strongest terms, is to delay this performance. If you proceed, you will endanger your health. I cannot give my consent."

He marked her medical notes with a flourish, clipped them to the foot of her bed and left the room without another word.

"Listen, I have everything planned," Josephine began to talk excitedly. "For the first night, I will just do three numbers. I'll start with 'J'ai Deux Amours' to show that I am French now and that I believe in Liberty, Equality and Fraternity, then a Negro lullaby to show I haven't forgotten my roots and I'll finish with a Gershwin tune to show the poetry of the American soul. Then a grand finale with the national anthems of France, USA and Britain." She looked more animated than she had done for a long time.

Jack knelt beside her, taking her hand. "I wish you wouldn't do this. But if you insist on going ahead, I'm with you every step of the way."

"Jack, my love. I couldn't do this without you."

That first performance at The Liberty Club before a non-segregated audience was watched by Moulay Larbi and Menebhi, who the Americans had flown from Marrakesh especially. Afterwards, the Americans held a grand reception at Grand Hotel Panoramique d'Anfa. Josephine arrived with Zimmer, Moulay Larbi and Menebhi. Despite having unhealed surgical scars on her stomach, she circulated amongst the guests, charming all. She had resumed the life of a star.

NEXT DAY

Zimmer greeted Josephine enthusiastically.

"I have some news which I hope you'll think is good. How are you feeling?"

Josephine smiled mischievously and winked. "Tell me."

"The Americans have asked me to arrange for you to do a tour for their troops. I am in charge of arrangements. They will supply transport and rations. We have fifteen days to organize and to give you an opportunity to recuperate."

"We'd better get started then."

Jack arrived at the palace and the place was buzzing. The servant who answered the door led him to a white bench with a cushion, placed before an ornate latticed grille sculpted from cedar wood which looked onto a courtyard. There he could see Menebhi's daughters bent over some of Josephine's costumes, sewing.

Menebhi joined him. "We're preparing to give a dinner in honor of Josephine, to celebrate her return to the stage."

Before he could clarify what on earth was going on, Josephine arrived in her customary whirlwind of excitement and hugged Jack.

"Come and see what's happening." Despite her thinness, she looked radiant. Her illness had been unable to rob her of her vitality.

"We leave in less than a week," she explained. "I have to go, Jack. It's for the American troops, and I have told them I won't perform in front of segregated audiences. All the performances will be free. No civilians."

Jack took her hand. "You shouldn't do this, you know that."

"I'll be careful, I promise," she replied with equal tenderness. "I just couldn't say no. Anyway, when we opened the storage trunks to check my stage costumes, some of them had been badly damaged by mites. Everyone is helping remake them."

Chapter 55

SOIREE AT PALACE MENEBHI, MARRAKESH

Jack arrived direct from Casablanca to attend the soiree at the palace. He was dressed in a dinner suit he had managed to borrow for the occasion and was looking forward to an exceptional evening. As he walked down the avenue of palm trees, he could see the entrance of the palace was guarded by two Berber guards, who gave every appearance of having come direct from the mountains. Their skin was leathered by exposure to the sun at high altitude. Both had narrow beards typical of their tribe. Their gleaming white jibbas were tied with red belts. Each held a magnificent silver saber and their expressions said they would not hesitate to use them.

As Jack was escorted into the banqueting hall, he could see that the majority of the gathered guests were men in uniform, mainly high-ranking American officers, although there were also ladies in sophisticated gowns and some men in tuxedos. Their hosts had surpassed themselves. The courtyard fountain had been trans-formed, water lilies floated on the surface of the pool and their petals fell with droplets of water as the fountain played. Dining tables were decorated with roses and laden with all manner of middle eastern delicacy. Subtle lighting illuminated the marble pillars, decorated with garlands of bougainvillea which surrounded the courtyard. Arab music echoed through the archways from a hidden minstrel's gallery.

His gaze locked onto Josephine as she wandered from one guest to another. A smile here, a nod there. She possessed the ability to effortlessly charm both men and women.

Although she was not the only beautiful woman present, she was the one that shone the brightest. She turned,

as if aware of his stare, and her face lit up with a smile as she beckoned him to join her. "Jack, thank goodness you've arrived," she said before continuing, "This is Colonel Archie Roosevelt, the son of the President. Archie, this is my captain and comrade in arms, Captain Jacques Abtey."

Later, one of the American soldiers commented loudly to his neighbor that he had "never sat down to eat with niggers before." An uncomfortable silence fell over the room as faces turned towards Menebhi. His eyes blazed with anger and he strode towards the offending soldier. Two Berber guards followed him with their hands on their sabers. The soldier sobered up as the implications of sparking a major diplomatic incident at this pivotal point in the war took hold. Josephine approached Menebhi and with her infectious charm soothed their fiercely proud host. After the meal, a troupe of Shilha dancers in exotic belly dancer costume entered the hall. Josephine got up to join them and then selected non-white men to join her and the dancers in a conga around the remaining guests as a very subtle snub to the racist soldier and anyone else present who might have shared his sentiments. After the dancers, the hall erupted with the sounds of American jazz. The party did not begin to wind down until four in the morning.

As guests began leaving, Jack was approached by a couple seeking directions to their hotel at the edge of the Arab Quarter. As it was virtually impossible to navigate the medina at night, Jack offered to guide them.

After escorting them to their hotel, he waved goodnight to them, but then found himself in compete darkness when he set out to return to the palace. He had forgotten to recover his electric torch from his companions and there was hardly any light whatsoever in the souks at night. What little glow there was from the stars was ineffective because of the overlapping roofs constructed to provide shade in the day, and a hiding place from the blistering sun. As he walked through the alleyways, he noticed a red orb of light ahead of him, just above head height.

Jack stopped as he approached what was clearly a ball of flame suspended in the air. The ball seemed to be guiding him, waiting until he approached before moving on. He was forced to consider whether he was hallucinating. As he stared more closely, he managed to discern the bare arms of a man who seemed to be controlling the ball of fire. Jack followed the fire and in no time at all found himself outside the palace.

When he explained his strange experience to Menebhi, he was told that the man who played with fire slept before the door of the palace at night. "He uses wood and coal for the fire, which he lights merely by blowing upon it. No one has ever seen him with a match or flint. There is no explanation for how he lights the fire. The man is homeless, but when we have tried to put him in a refuge, he always returns. We feed him, not that he eats much. He's one of the mysteries of our country."

Giraud, the French General who had collaborated with the Germans and then, after the North Africa landings, switched his support to the Allies, appeared to be a candidate to lead the Free French troops. Jack was infuriated that de Gaulle's position as leader seemed in jeopardy. Reluctant to take orders through Giraud, he forged a pass to enable him fly to London in order to liaise directly with de Gaulle.

Meantime, Josephine organized a performance at the Cinema Rialto Casablanca. Jack returned after the performance and found that Josephine and Zimmer had been refused sandwiches by the American troops and had not eaten since the previous day. Jack was angered, but Josephine laughed it off. "We are really on the straw now, isn't it magnificent."

Chapter 56

CASABLANCA, MARCH 1943

When Jack returned from his mission, he went immediately to the hall where preparations were underway for the first gala for the French Red Cross.

Josephine took his hand, gazing into his eyes she said, "Don't worry, I have waited for you, but be patient and don't take offence if I don't make a fuss over you. I have been ill for so long and it's rejuvenating to be in the public eye. I have a purpose again."

Jack left her to prepare for her first gala and found Zimmer under a mountain of French flags with which he was trying to decorate the reception hall, a room rapidly being transformed as a result of his efforts.

"Have you got any money? We could not eat at lunch time."

"What? Do you mean Josephine hasn't eaten either? "He reached into his pocket and gave Zimmer all the money he had to buy food.

"Thanks," Zimmer said with feeling.

"This has to stop," Jack said. "She still hasn't fully recovered from her operations."

"Don't worry, this performance should raise enough money to support the rest of the tour. We're very lucky, We've been able to rescue Fred Rey from an internment camp and he is going to join us on the tour. We will perform at the American Base in Oran as the first leg of the tour of American camps."

"Please try and make sure she doesn't exhaust herself. "

"I will try. She is inspiring. I have seen soldiers cry when she sings 'J'ai Deux Amours' as the finale of her performance.

Chapter 57

ORAN

There were three hundred thousand men in camps, in barracks or tents for thirty kilometers around Oran. Josephine and her team were given a jeep and performed several times a day.

An orchestra of black soldiers had been trained to accompany the sets. They ended the program with "It's a Long Way to Tipperary" and the three national anthems.

One evening, the performance took place in the middle of a field with projectors used to provide light. In the middle of "J'ai Deux Amours," German fighter planes swooped down on the crowd and machine gun bullets ripped up the turf as the soldiers either took cover or took up their positions on defensive guns.

Josephine remained standing, using the break to sample some of the ice cream on offer. With the second swoop from the fighter planes, the trail of bullets landed closer to her and she dived to the ground under one of the tables.

"Watch out for your teeth," Zimmer yelled, knowing how much she valued them.

Josephine immediately covered her mouth with her hand. Once the plane passed by, she stood up, dusted down her dress and commented, "Never mind my teeth, this dress cost nineteen hundred francs and I've been crawling about in the sand in it." Then she yelled out to the band to get back in position so they could finish the show.

At Mostaganem, the population of mainly Italian and Spanish origin was hostile, and Josephine arranged a public performance in the square. She and the soldiers mingled in the crowd giving sweets to the women and children, and cigarettes to men in an attempt to create a friendly ambiance.

As usual, Josephine charmed all. The tour continued for four weeks, after which Josephine returned to Marrakesh.

Chapter 58

LIBYA, JUNE 1943

Jack was waiting to wrap a blanket around her as she descended from the jeep. His eyes filled with sadness as he watched her limp from stiffness over to the camp chair which he had unfolded for her. He knew that if he asked how she was; she would answer brightly with a smile. But he had stopped asking because he feared even the extra energy that took to put on a show for him was draining for her, and she needed every ounce of strength she had.

For weeks he had been trying to persuade her to rest even for a few days. He could see the toll on her health. Although her smile remained as bright as ever she seemed more drained after each performance-although when she was on stage or on whatever passed for such, no-one in the audience could have guessed how feeble she really was.

Always her response was the same.

"How can you suggest that? Can the soldiers rest? No, we must go on."

So, the kilometers rolled away as the jeep tires spun. He drove one jeep, Josephine the other. But the days under the fierce Sahara sun were grueling and the cold nights in army tents in the unforgiving terrain were worse.

Whilst the risks from attack had now diminished with the surrender of the Afrika corps there was still risks of falling foul of the land mines which scattered the desert, or one of the groups of bandits which wandered across the dunes on camels like pirates at sea.

The desert itself was dangerous, nature at its most

beautiful and most dangerous. Capable, at any moment of luring the unwary to a lingering death.

Jack lit a fire with scrub they had gathered on the way, and as darkness fell, they crouched around the flames gulping down a tin of spam each from their ration packs for dinner.

Sand seemed to have become part of him. It was in his food, his hair, every crease and crevice of his body. They had to endure just one more night before they reached Egypt, where they would hopefully be afforded the luxury of a shower. He brought his camp chair beside her and began to massage her shoulders.

He felt her body relax then tense again as hyenas barking and howled in the distance, the sound carrying like a ghostly warning across the desert dunes.

"It's nearly over," he said. Now that the Germans have been driven out of North Africa, it is only a matter of time. We will be able to rest in Cairo.

"It's not that," she stuttered. "It's those boys' faces. I can see them in my head. Last week, even yesterday, they were happy, laughing and joking. In the next few days, they might be lying dead. Struck by Nazi gunfire or burned to death in a tank they had no hope of escaping from. I feel like I'm deceiving them. Giving them hope when there is none. When they should just turn and run."

"You know how much your performances mean to the soldiers, Josephine."

"But this information we gather: troop movements, tank deployment. I know what's going to happen and I can't tell them. I can't warn them. It twists me inside. I know more about where they are going to be sent than they do. What right have I to keep secrets?"

"I'm sorry ..."

"It's too hard." She was wailing now as her emotions took hold. "What chance have these boys got for the landings that are coming? I feel like they are being sent to their deaths, and I am standing by the roadside cheering them on."

Jack stroked her back. Trying to comfort her with his

touch. "Come here, my darling," he said wrapping her in his arms and gently rocking her. How frail she had become. He could feel her bones outlined against her flesh. He knew she should not be travelling, but how could he stop her. The need to entertain the troops was her driving force. But it was also grueling. She was performing several times a day in front of thousands of troops on makeshift stages.

And travelling by jeep across the desert between performances, living on rations and sleeping close to the jeep at night for fear of landmines all took its toll. He stroked her hair and thought how much he loved her. Everything about her. Her passion. Her determination. Her whole crazy self in its entirety.

"You *are* making a difference, Josephine. How many people can say that? And it can't last forever. Now that the Americans are involved, it is only a matter of time."

"But how many more lives ... How many more young men will be sentenced to a pointless death? I can't bear it."

Chapter 59

ALGIERS

"What are your plans now?" the major asked as he closed the door.

Jack shrugged his shoulders. "I'd expected to be posted to join the landing forces. We both know that Josephine's work for the Bureau of Information must come to an end. There' no question of her attempting a mission in France now. It would be madness. My secondment as her assistant presumably will end. Why, sir?"

"We have other plans for you both," the major sat down opposite Jack at the desk with its pen and ink and paper as meticulously ordered as its user.

"While we can be confident the war will be won," the major shrugged and gestured with his hands, "it is only a matter of time. The Germans will be beaten back until they surrender. But the situation here in North Africa is volatile. Now that the danger across North Africa from the Germans has gone, our old troubles are resurfacing. We need your services and those of Josephine for a little bit longer. What do you think?"

Jack sat back, puzzled. "What exactly do you have in mind?"

The major flipped open the manila folder in front of him and took out some sheets of paper with photographs attached. "We need to know what's going on. These individuals are inciting revolt against

French sovereignty now we have chased the Nazis out for them. You and Josephine, with your contacts, are ideally placed to report on the Arabs."

"You want us to spy on our friends?"

"No. We need to safeguard French interests in our territories here. We need to exercise diplomacy and common sense. Otherwise, we'll be embroiled in another war before we've defeated the Germans. We must avoid a crisis in Africa. Old rivalries are resurfacing. We believe with the unique contacts and trust which you and Josephine have built up here that you are ideally qualified for this role. I can't pretend that it won't be difficult or dangerous." The major added more seriously, "Volunteers only."

"We've always put the interests of France first in our liaisons with the Arabs."

"That is understood. We are asking you both to become adventurers for the French heritage. Your role is to see, meet, discuss and find an equitable solution to the problems that are out there."

Chapter 60

ALGIERS, 15 JULY 1943

Jack was relieved when Josephine returned. He had been burning to discuss the new role proposed for them. Not least because it would mean they would not be separated as he had expected. Josephine hugged him when he told her. "Thank goodness, we can stay together, and you will have an active role. It's terrible to leave a man like you inactive, it's like leaving you with your hands in your pockets and your mouth open to catch flies. I want to do this, Jack. I know many of the Arabs, their attitudes, the way their minds work."

She continued, eyes sparkling, "While I was in Egypt, I met an attaché from the British Embassy. The British are taking a great interest in what's going on here at the moment. This attaché had been invited to a meeting in Beirut. The situation between the French sailors stationed there and British soldiers was tense. The French are suspicious of the British who they think are planning to take over their role in post-war North Africa. I gave a performance in Beirut and was received by the French Ambassador there. The general impression I got from him was that the British are quite ready to install themselves in the Middle East and may not wait until Germany's been totally defeated. I also made some other useful contacts."

"Go on ..."

"The Director of the Egyptian Ministry of Foreign Affairs. One evening, I was dining at the Pavilion de Chasse Royale in Cairo. I was approached by the manager who said that King Farouk would like me to sing for him. I told him that I couldn't possibly do that. When the manager came back it was to say, 'Mademoiselle, it is not a request that you sing, it is an order. You do not refuse a king.'

I told him that I was very flattered to receive the order, and if His Majesty would like to arrange a suitable evening, I would be delighted to perform. I thought the matter was closed and I went onto the floor to dance with my dining companion."

"Let me guess, the English attaché," Jack interrupted sharply.

Josephine continued as if she had not noticed the jealously in his voice. "I began dancing. The king instructed the orchestra to stop playing and a police officer sent by the manager told me to leave. I told them I was not going to leave. I had gone there to dance, so I began dancing, but the police officer insisted I leave. I told him I was very annoyed at the way his majesty was behaving. Anyway," she continued, ignoring Jack's expression. "The following day, the Foreign Affairs Minister agreed to put on a concert at the Theatre Royal in Cairo with me in aid of Franco–Egyptian friendship. As you know, the situation between the provisional government of France and the Egyptians is very delicate as they wish to maintain their neutrality in the conflict. The representative of Marshal Pétain has stopped exercising control, support for de Gaulle is mixed, and some French are not sure about fighting alongside the British. Everything is very unstable. Investors not certain of outcome of the war want to ensure they finish on the winning side. King Farouk will attend the performance. I have to make the arrangements. But it will fit in perfectly with our new mission." Josephine finished enthusiastically and Jack agreed. It was impossible not to be infected by her enthusiasm.

They relaxed, sipping whiskies as Josephine relayed her other news. She had sung at an immense airbase near the Arch of the Philaeni, which the English called Marble Arch, built by Mussolini in Libya on the border between the areas of Tripolitania and Cyrenaica.

In Cairo, she had sang in all the camps for half an hour, four or five times per day.

She had visited "boomtown," a city of tents which the Americans had created in the sand, and performed at a Free Belgian unit. She had met Vivienne Leigh and Noel Coward, who had said it was not possible to find a better ambassador for the troops than Miss Baker. She had visited hospitals to meet with the injured of El Alamein, Mersa Matruh, Sollum, Tobruk and Bir Hakeim to offer soothing words of comfort and encouragement.

Chapter 61

ALGIERS, COLONEL
BILLOTTE'S OFFICE

"Felicitations, Josephine," he said. "Your tour has been a triumph. Good reports from everyone. The morale of the troops is markedly boosted by your performances and visits, and you are perfectly qualified for the next role. I am sure Jack has explained what I have in mind. It will take perhaps two weeks to organize the administrative formalities. You can have a few days of recuperation. I cannot thank you enough." He shook her hand.

She and Jack would organize a series of performances in the Middle East, but the secrecy of the true intent of the operation was paramount. Officially, the group (Josephine, Zimmer, Fred and Jack as chief) was making a propaganda tour to raise funds for the French resistance under the patronage of General de Gaulle. The initial performance was scheduled for the Théâtre Municipal of Algiers. The proceeds would fund the rest of the tour.

They travelled through towns in jeeps painted the color of sand with the Cross of Lorraine emblazoned in red on the bonnets, which attracted the curious attention of the people used to seeing the khaki green of American vehicles.

In Marrakesh, Menebhi gave a feast in their honor, and the

friends sat on cushions around a large table with everyone chatting, eating and drinking.

It was there the idea was born that Menehbi should join them on their mission. His father was known throughout the world of Islam, and his presence would inevitably open doors which would otherwise be closed. He was a supporter of de Gaulle and believed that he would be able to deal with the issues and evolution of the French protectorate.

Jack pondered. "I need to think about it, Josephine. It's a good idea, but you mustn't forget that he, like his father, is protected by the British. I can see objections from above. And we would have to wait for four days for him to obtain a visa and we are due to leave, unless of course I add him onto my order of mission as an interpreter. And it's another person in the jeep. You could travel by airplane, I suppose."

"I want to travel with you."

Jack laughed. "Why not, it drives through all four wheels and has a powerful engine. But, again I must remind you, it's seventeen hundred kilometers from here to Algiers."

Three days later, they left Marrakesh. What a sight. Jack, Josephine and Menebhi in the front with the back seat piled high with kitbags and suitcases. Balanced on top was the jeep driver who had become a passenger. That evening, they spent the night in Fez as guests of an uncle of Menebhi. After a delicious meal, they slept for the night on cushions in a huge reception room where below the floor they could hear an underground stream.

They drove in terrible heat the next day to reach de Gaulle. Menebhi met him that evening and was very taken with the General.

He told Jack and Josephine, "My father, the grand Vizier of Sultan Moulay Abd al-Aziz, was very much in favor of Morocco becoming a British protectorate and it was a result of that that the King of England gave him title of Sir. When, however, it became a French protectorate, he maintained a good relationship with the French officials. It always remained his opinion that the best interests of Morocco would be served if she were under the British.

I am not superstitious, and I do not attach undue importance to dreams, but last night, I dreamed that I was in the palace of Tangier in the reception hall attending a family reunion over which my father presided. Suddenly, he rose from his seat and began to walk towards me, holding a flag in French colors and a bundle of keys.

It is my belief that my father has shown me the future. Now that I have met de Gaulle, I am ready to put my trust in him."

Jack and Josephine glanced at each other. Their mission, if it continued as it had begun, would be a success.

Chapter 62

ALGIERS, WINTER 1943

"We must have a flag."

Jack laughed, "What are you talking about?".

Josephine was in high spirits. In just three days she had managed to compile a sixty-piece jazz band from American soldiers to accompany her performance. The first concert that evening would be in aid of the Free French Forces and de Gaulle would be in the audience with his wife.

"A flag for the Free French Forces. We must have one."

Jack shook his head. He could never predict from which direction Josephine's ideas would fly at him next. One moment, a child; the next, world peace. Once she had something in her head, there was no stopping her. Hadn't their lives over the past few years proved that a thousand times?

"Yes, we must have one for tonight, for de Gaulle." She flashed him a determined look that told him this was not a matter for debate.

"Even if we could find suitable material, there is no time to sew it."

"Yes, it will be the flag of France with the Cross of Lorraine. I know," she snapped her fingers in his face. "I can borrow the jeep."

"Remember how little fuel we have," he called after her. This was another mission he wasn't going to try and interfere with. Josephine disappeared. She knew she could persuade some of her friends to part with some cloth. Red, white and blue material would not be too difficult to find, and as for nimble fingers to do the sewing, Josephine knew just who to ask.

Less than an hour later, the jeep screeched to a halt outside the Nunnery of the Sacred Order. Josephine pounded at the weathered oak door until a nun clad entirely in white answered. With rolls of cloth in her arms, Josephine charmed an audience with the Mother Superior. Twenty minutes later as the convent door closed behind her, the nuns were being summoned to their new task by the ringing of bells.

The concert was a triumph. At the intermission, it was the proudest moment of her life when Josephine received a message to join the de Gaulles on the balcony. The General stood up and gave Josephine his chair. She found herself making small talk with Madame de Gaulle.

Finally, the General took his own gold Cross of Lorraine from his lapel and presented it to her. "Mademoiselle, France salutes you. Let me give you this cross as a small token of thanks from myself and the French nation."

At the encore, Josephine returned to the stage, and at her signal, the huge flag with the Cross of Lorraine dropped from ceiling to floor. The audience, including de Gaulle, stood up to give a standing ovation. Josephine looked up to him and curtsied to her hero.

Chapter 63

TUNISIA

Typically, Zimmer had organized the performances in Tunisia with a master's hand. Having decided to travel to Tunisia by jeep, they left Algiers at six in the evening. The jeep, piled high with bags, was followed by a big Hotchkiss. They travelled through the mountains of Kabyle in Northern Algeria driving non-stop to arrive more quickly. However, they had forgotten their map and took a wrong turn onto a minor road.

Finally, they arrived at the Tunisian border, but at a section where the tracks were difficult and dangerous. For nearly two hours their route ran alongside the edge of a ravine of indeterminate depth. Sparse vegetation and rocky cliffs created a bizarre landscape evocative of a magnificent spectral scene. The Hotchkiss had to be abandoned after breaking an axle on the unforgiving path, and their luggage had to be stacked precariously onto the jeep. Throughout the latter part of the journey they travelled through regions battered by combat.

Villages destroyed. Bridges burned. Fields bombed. In the last fifty kilometers of the journey, the jeep's engine gave up and they finished their journey to Tunis being towed. The port was in reasonable condition, and thankfully, Zimmer had reserved nice rooms.

Josephine organized shows for three days. The proceeds from the first two days were designated for the French resistance, and the third day's tally went for French and Allied troops, but the tension between the troops was tangible. Before leaving, they visited Sfax, a town which had been destroyed, and the surviving inhabitants were camping in the

ruins of their city.

Josephine distributed chocolate from their rations to the children who danced and laughed with her despite their surroundings.

The next stage of their journey was the 3,500 kilometer trek to Cairo. After some discussion, Jack organized the appropriation of three new jeeps. As he collected them late in the evening, he was warned to take care of the freshly painted sand-colored vehicles.

They left Tunis at two in the morning, travelling on back roads to avoid American troops searching for three missing jeeps. The first jeep carried their bags, then Jack driving with Josephine and Menebhi as passengers, behind them were Fred and the drivers.

The following day, they passed the Mareth Line, which had been the defensive line between the British and the Afrika Korps. They visited an oasis for lunch and were able to swim in the clear water while naked children offered them dates and red peppers. They stopped briefly at the Souara cemetery for the Free French Forces, finally arriving in Tripoli late in the evening. They were having difficulty finding something to eat or anywhere to stay. Eventually, they stopped outside a large hotel on the jetty and Josephine and Jack went together to look for the British officer in charge.

"It's impossible to provide accommodation," the officer informed them.

"But this is ridiculous. Don't you recognize Josephine Baker? She has given tours for your troops. We have just come from a performance for the benefit of Allied soldiers," Jack said as he produced his order, and the officer examined Josephine from all angles.

"I can make a room available for Miss Baker," the officer said. "In fact, why don't you join me and my fellow officers. We are having a celebration in the hotel."

Josephine rolled her eyes at Jack and addressed the officer. "Can't you even give them some food?"

"No." the officer replied firmly.

Josephine decided to refuse the officer's offer, but her companions persuaded her to accept for two reasons: she would have the benefit of a good night's rest, which was vital in view of her health, and she would be able to bring them some sandwiches. Jack and the others spent the night lying on the paving stones in the hotel courtyard beside the vehicles.

The following day, Jack set out at seven in the morning to obtain food supplies for the next leg of their journey, a distance of nine hundred kilometers. He was advised by the French that there were no supplies, so he went next to the British army supply post.

On presentation of his orders, Jack was supplied with the exact rations needed for their journey: seven days' rations and fuel for the three-hundred kilometers to the next fuel stop. Jack was anxious about the supplies.

The tribesmen could cross the Sahara guided by the shape of the dunes, the smell of the vegetation, the stars, the location of the sun and the moon in the sky, and the positioning of camel dung, but he just had a compass. A sandstorm or vehicle breakdown could prove disastrous. Their supplies allowed no margin for problems and delays on the journey.

Tripoli was surrounded by an oasis of palm trees, which could be seen from a distance. They made good time and stopped at Homs to admire the Roman ruins there. As they marveled at the extraordinary buildings which had been constructed, they were also conscious of how the once great city had virtually disappeared into the sand, swallowed by the desert.

By afternoon, they had reached Misurata, a little Italian village perched on the shores of the Mediterranean, where the houses were abandoned, and the beaches were lined with signs indicating mines.

Sixty kilometers later the road became virtually impassable, pitted by tank bombardment. Aware of the severe risk of mines at nightfall, they searched for a stony area to make camp.

Alerted by a sound in the night, Jack woke and saw two men circling their camp. He rose silently, collected his gun from the jeep and sat cross-legged and alert as the scavengers slipped away into the night. After that, they took turns at keeping guard.

As they drove through the desert of Syrtes, they were shocked by the depressing evidence of recent battles, crashed airplanes and burned-out tanks, military clothes and equipment, scattered over the landscape like the carelessly abandoned toys of giant children. They drove on, anxious to leave the desert. Around midnight, they were halted by British Military Police who examined their orders.

"Well, we can allow you to continue, but you do realize that this area is designated as dangerous because of the mines. You are at risk of being blown up if you stray from the center of the road. True, some areas have been cleaned and designated safe, but it will be impossible for you to determine these areas at night. We'd prefer that you return with us to our barracks and spend the night with us."

It was an offer they were unable to refuse. In honor of their visitors, the policemen produced the best of their rations. Meeting them by chance in the middle of the desert, had been a stoke of good luck. The policemen were as relaxed and welcoming as if they had stopped for tea in their native Hampshire – uniforms exemplary, gleaming white gloves and gaiters, ammunition boots waxed and polished until they shone. In the infernal heat, they operated traffic control as if they were in Piccadilly, London.

Benghazi, Derna, Tobruk, – the ruins of the cities rolled past.

Chapter 64

TOBRUK

They camped just outside Tobruk. That night they were woken by cries of "Stop, Stop! Captain, we are lost. We are drowning." Jack lit his kerosene lamp and could see the young sailor who had been assigned to their group on his elbows between Josephine and Menebhi, his eyes fixed ahead. Josephine was already awakened and took his hand. Then in a soothing voice she repeated, "My dear. You know that we are on land. Rest ... sleep ..." until he fell asleep. When he woke, he could remember nothing.

On leaving Tobruk, they found themselves again driving through a part of the desert where two armies had fought viciously to the death. Abandoned tanks with Nazi insignias were stranded on dunes. Twisted metal poked from the sand in contorted shapes. The desolate aftermath of battle gave the travelers the sense of driving through an endless graveyard.

Irritated by a remark Jack made during a lunch stop, Josephine set off at high speed in Jack's jeep. She was not accustomed to driving the vehicle, which had sensitive steering and could be erratic in the hands of an inexperienced driver. Jack followed slowly in another jeep because he knew she would drive faster and as a consequence more dangerously if she believed he was trying to catch up with her.

The track twisted up through the mountains, dangerous ravines fell off to one side. Finally, when her temper had cooled, she stopped at the top of a mountain pass. When Jack pulled up beside her, she was sitting cross-armed in the jeep. With her face sullen and still wearing her bonnet and goggles, she looked like a comic figure. Menebhi, her unlucky passenger, jumped out of the jeep with relief.

"I had my throat in my mouth. I never thought I would see my home again. The more I begged her to stop, the harder she pressed on the accelerator. Please drive."

Jack jumped into the driving seat and Josephine stalked off and climbed into the second jeep.

Around one hundred kilometers before Alexandria, they paused to examine an abandoned German aircraft. Josephine and Jack reconciled, and she again joined him in his jeep. Jack set off leading their convoy. Barely an hour later, they heard yells. Jack slammed on the brakes and the jeep came to an abrupt halt. They turned to see the second jeep rolling as if in slow motion down the hillside. It turned three times before landing on its wheels and coming to a stop. Two of the passengers were flung from the vehicle like dolls. They scrambled down the hillside. When they reached the vehicle, Fred and the driver were moving, but the sailor lay lifeless where he had been thrown. In shock, Jack and Josephine set off to find help.

They found a driver to return to the scene of the accident. No one could explain what had caused it. The track was in good condition. Somehow the jeep had slipped off the track. Menebhi and Fred travelled to Alexandria with the dead sailor in a car summoned by the Military Police. The police arranged treatment for the injured driver.

When night came, Jack and Josephine drove towards Alexandria. They were still in shock and hungry as they had not eaten. Jack had been so exhausted that for the last fifty kilometers, he had asked Josephine to drive. In the moonlight, the tragic suffering in her face had been all too apparent. When they finally arrived in Alexandria, they searched for their friends in the streets.

They found them in the morning at the military hospital where they had been detained because Jack was still in possession of their orders. They all stayed in Alexandria for three days. The sailor was taken to the Military Cemetery where he was buried after a simple ceremony amongst other members of the Free French Forces. The tragic death of their

comrade impacted them all, the young man had been looking forward to returning to France and the future he had planned for after the war. It was not to be.

In Alexandria, Menebhi had resumed his traditional clothing. Prince Mohammed Ali invited Menebhi to visit his summer residence, and Jack was invited to join them. Menebhi told the prince that they were on a mission on behalf of General de Gaulle. After exchange of family news, they turned their discussion to politics. Menebhi explained that in his view France had an important role to play in the Middle East because of the possibility of a union with the Arab peoples.

The prince had a request. "Ask General de Gaulle how important he considers it for France to be active in the discussions between the different Arab peoples. Does he want to see French interests in North Africa end? The French must realize it is important they act quickly to defend their interests in the Middle East.

In principle, we still want France in the Middle East, but there must be fairness and balance." Then the prince set out to explain his vision in detail and charged Menebhi and Jack with taking his message to de Gaulle, reminding them finally that he was both an Arab and a Frenchman.

As soon as Jack and Menebhi returned from the palace, the group left for Cairo. The date for the grand fete in Egypt to be attended by King Farouk was fixed for the end of October. This was a great diplomatic coup. Josephine explained she had a giant French flag with the Cross of Lorraine, but she was warned not to use it at the gala.

They arrived in Lebanon for their show on the same night as the national elections. It was an eventful night. In the Grand Hotel de

Sofar, Josephine decided to auction off her gold Cross of Lorraine, which raised 3,500 francs.

The injured and sick at the military hospital where Josephine had sung earlier in the day donated 30,000 francs for the resistance.

In total, the whole evening raised almost one million francs. The pro-French candidate won the election, and the following day Menebhi was received by the new Lebanese President, then by the President of the Syrian Republic. As a goodwill token, they were provided with a government car when they left Damascus for Jerusalem.

One car followed the other. Josephine, Jack and Menebhi departed in the first vehicle leaving Fred and two Foreign Legionnaires, who performed a comic sketch in their show, and their driver to follow them. As Jack drove towards Lake Tiberias, a motorcyclist caught up with them and flagged them down. There had been an accident, he told them. The second car had overturned. More than that, he could not say.

Filled with dread, Josephine, Jack and Menebhi turned around and drove back the way they had come. Soon they saw the car overturned with its wheels in the air. A protruding rock was the only obstacle which had prevented the vehicle from plunging into the ravine that bordered the road. Sitting in the grass beside the car were the legionnaires and Fred, calmly smoking cigars. The driver had been concussed and was taken by ambulance to hospital. Another car was dispatched for their use. Fred decided to join Jack and the others in their car.

Later that day, they arrived in Jerusalem where rooms had been reserved for them at the King David Hotel. They collapsed on their beds, fully clothed.

From the hotel balcony, it was possible to see the ancient city, the mountains of Galilee and over the Jordan Valley to the Dead Sea. Josephine was impressed with the Sacred City and stayed long into the night gazing at the stars. Jack too was affected by the atmosphere of this ancient place, feeling great sadness and desolation. As the moon climbed high in the night sky lighting the city and valleys with mystery, he returned several times to contemplate his surroundings and to meditate.

Josephine decided to hold a soiree in the hotel and then a show in the cinema of the old town. She was approached by Jews from Palestine who wanted to interview her about the temporary government in France and the intrigues of the Middle East, but she was careful to maintain a diplomatic stance in her conversations with the press.

Despite the performances and intelligence-gathering duties, they managed to visit the old city and the Dead Sea, where they laughed and joked as they floated on the dense, salty water. They finished the tour with visits to Tel Aviv and Haifa. Everywhere they went, they raised the flag of the Free French Forces, raised money for the resistance groups and tried to demonstrate France's good intentions so far as the future of North Africa was concerned.

Meantime, the Arab Union expressed an intention to eliminate France from Libya and Syria.

The Grand Soiree Franco–Egyptian was to take place at the L'Opera Royale in Cairo. While King Farouk agreed to attend, they were forbidden to use the flag in case of shocking his majesty. Because of the politically delicate situation, it was decided that the show would be in aid of the children of France. Josephine was incensed by the instruction not to use her flag and decided to establish contact with the king through an intermediary. His reply was direct.

"In accepting the invitation, I have not ignored that the gala is in honor of Free French Forces and I would not be surprised if it proceeded under the flag of the Free French."

"There," she said, waving the note at Jack. "I told you we could use the flag."

Chapter 65

CAIRO

Jack watched closely as Josephine dabbed the side of her mouth with her napkin. She had seemed edgy over dinner.

"Are you feeling all right?"

"I've got a bit of a headache. I think I'll just go up to my room now. You don't mind, do you?"

"Let me come with you."

"No, really I think I could do with some time on my own. We can catch up properly tomorrow."

"If that's what you want," he said, a bit huffed. He had been looking forward to spending the night with her. He watched as she walked away. Her body swayed in that elegant way she had, holding his attention until she reached the stairs. As she reached the foot of the stairway, her movements changed and she started to run up the stairs with surprising energy.

"Damn that woman," he thought, as he got up throwing down his napkin and following her. When he reached her door, it was closed. He listened, but he couldn't hear anything. Perhaps he had been mistaken. He tapped sharply on the door several times, but there was no answer. He tapped again. "Josephine. Josephine," he called. "Do you want me to break the door down?"

The door opened a crack and her face peeped out. "I don't want to see you right now. Go away, please." She went to close the door, but he jammed his foot in the space preventing her from doing so. Then as he forced the door open the British attaché was revealed, standing behind Josephine. She was naked apart from her high-heeled sandals. The man was hastily buttoning his shirt.

Jack reached out and slapped Josephine so hard she fell backwards on the bed. Jack turned to the man. "You want some?" He raised his hand ready to strike, but the man lowered his eyes and shouldered past Jack. His steps echoed as he ran down the stairs.

"What the hell do you think you're playing at?" he shouted at her.

"Me? What the hell do *you* think you're playing at?" she yelled as she stood up.

"You promised me. No adventures."

"He's on the same side as us."

"No, Josephine. We can't trust anyone. Don't think I don't know that the British have tried to get you to spy for them."

"If he'd hit you, I'd have left with him."

"I know," Jack retorted. "And it would have been no more than I deserved. But he didn't, did he?"

They both stood facing each other, breathing hard and glaring.

"Are you all right? I shouldn't have hit you. I think about how dangerous it is for you. I think about Mata Hari. She was shot for sleeping with a German. There was no evidence that she gave him any information. She might even have been obtaining information for the French. I couldn't bear for something to happen to you."

Josephine shrugged, calmer but still angry. "He's British. Where's the harm?"

Jack shook his head. "Everything is so delicate at the moment. We can't risk any upsets."

"You know that even though we're on the same side, the British and Americans spy on us and we spy on them," she said.

"You promised me that you wouldn't sleep with anyone else, not while we are working undercover together."

She nodded. "I know."

But she turned, looking at him defiantly, and said, "The promise was for France, not for you. Do you understand?"

He nodded.

She ran her hand along her cheek where he had hit her. "This war won't last forever." She held the door open. "Now get out."

He walked out of the room, and she slammed the door behind him. As she sat down on the bed, she knew Jack should have reported her for liaising with the attaché. She knew she had promised no adventures. It wasn't that she didn't love Jack or even that he didn't satisfy her. Quite the contrary. It was just the not knowing. An experience missed. An opportunity lost. The Englishman had attracted her with his athletic body, his vitality and his youth. She had found no reason not to satisfy her curiosity.

NEXT DAY

Jack ran after her. "Come with me."

"No, I'm driving the other jeep."

"If you were a man, I would have shot you."

She whirled round, eyes blazing. "If I'd had a gun, I would have shot *you*. I can still feel where you hit me."

"But you know how dangerous this is. Do you think you would be treated differently than Mata Hari?"

She challenged him. "Do you think I'm a traitor?"

He took her face in his hands and stared into her eyes with all the depth of his soul.

"You, ma chérie, are more royal than a king, more French than Napoléon. But this is a war and should suspicion fall on you ..."

Josephine laughed. "Maybe I found something that might be useful."

She took out from her pocket a piece of paper with her distinctive handwriting scrawled on it. She swung it slowly in front of his eyes. "What do you think this is?"

Jack shrugged.

"My notes. Would you like to know what I found out?"

He reached for the paper. "You're incorrigible."

Josephine whipped back her hand and stuffed the note back in her pocket.

"Not until you apologize properly."

"You don't need to do this for France."

She laughed again. "This," she said, pulling out the note again and waving it in front of his eyes. "I did for France. The Englishman, I did for me!"

With that she turned sharply without waiting for his reaction and headed for the jeep.

Their last days in Cairo were very interesting. They were assigned a local guide who, through his extensive contacts, was able to take them not only to the pyramids but to places they would never otherwise have seen. They visited a brotherhood of Dervish Moslems following a religious path of poverty and austerity in the mountains. They toured remote fortresses with military guards and saw prison cells dug out from the rock.

What a spectacle they made when they finally pulled out of Cairo. They were a veritable quartet of clowns perched in a jeep which appeared as if it could fall apart at any moment. They had tried to tie the front bumper in place but it still hung lopsided, the roll bar was dented and one of the front headlights was smashed. A reconciled Josephine, wrapped in a navy-blue Royal Air Force overcoat she had managed to purchase in the market and wearing Jack's hat with some oversized motorbike goggles, sat in the front passenger seat. Beside her, Jack, driving, wearing yellow gloves, which reached to his elbows, a woolen hat and an old army jacket. In the back, Zimmer sported an outlandish jacket and knitted hat, whilst Menebhi wore two coats with a khaki sleeping bag over the top. They could have easily been mistaken for vagabonds. And what an assortment of characters! Josephine, an infamous black American who prayed devoutly as both a Jew and a Christian; Jack, a Free French Soldier of French stock raised in the Catholic faith; Zimmer, a man of talent and mystery; and Menebhi, Muslim

royalty under the protectorate of the British crown.

But in spite of their differences, it was their belief in the principles of Liberty, Equality and Fraternity which had drawn them together and bound them so tightly. They were a true band of brothers, closer than blood relatives. As the jeep bounced along over potholes, they laughed and joked. Their mission had been successful and the tour had raised over three million francs. They would have a great deal to report when they reached their destination.

Jack glanced across at Josephine. Her face was animated. Her performances had been a triumph. The intelligence gathering of considerable value. His heart swelled with emotion as he reflected on the months they had spent together in North Africa. They were truly soldiers subject to the fortunes of war, one moment thrown together like pebbles tossed on a beach, the next driven apart as the waves rolled on, too insignificant to have any effect on the tide. He wondered what future waited for them on their return to Marrakesh. As with all the other questions that plagued his thoughts, he had no answers.

Chapter 66

ALGIERS, 18 NOVEMBER 1943

Commandant Brousset leaned forward over his desk and looked at Jack intently. "Glad to have you back. Sit down and tell me your news."

"You will have my full report later this morning."

"I should tell you that I have received a complaint regarding your conduct and a request that you receive a formal reprimand."

Jack paused. "What exactly is the complaint, sir?"

"Well, it originates from the Egyptian Foreign Affairs Minister for Free France and it concerns the performance of a certain sketch and ignoring an instruction not to display a certain flag."

Jack laughed. The Commandant laughed too. "I expect that the information you'll provide in your report will allow me to dispose of this complaint in an appropriate manner." He scrunched up the piece of paper and threw it in the wastepaper bin beside his desk.

"Don't worry, I will defend your position to the end. I know the spirit in which you departed."

When Jack returned to the Hotel Regina, an irate Josephine was packing their belongings into bags.

"Can you believe it, Jack? The hotel manager told me we have to get out. This morning. The hotel has been requisitioned and this room will be converted into a dormitory."

"You won't believe what happened to me this morning," Jack answered. "Don't worry. I'll arrange accommodation for us with the army."

Jack explained to the quartermasters he required accommodation for himself, Josephine and Menebhi.

"For you, no problem, but the others, no, they are not officers."

Jack refused the offer of a room for him alone. Commandant Moynet offered to share his room, and that is where they billeted for the night, sleeping on the floor. The following night, a doctor offered them a room within his practice. Josephine slept on the bed and the others slept on the metallic tables in the consulting room.

The following day, Jack received further orders at a meeting with Billotte.

"The situation between France and Britain over Suez is becoming increasingly explosive. It's imperative that you both see the General."

As this involved a two-week wait, they decided to return to Marrakesh.

Chapter 67

MARRAKESH, NOVEMBER 1943

They ran out of fuel just outside the city, but finally they arrived at Menebhi's palace, where they were joyously received, and steps put in place immediately to prepare a welcome feast for the following day. During the night, the noise of the preparations continued as couscous was prepared together with other delicacies.

The Americans and British were now making a great deal of noise about the Atlantic Charter, originally drawn up in secret before the US entered the war, but by 1943, an important political declaration of the Allied war aims.

It was being interpreted as offering the establishment of independent Arab states across the Mahgreb once the war with Germany was concluded, and was therefore a time bomb from a French perspective. Jack was forced to return to Algiers, leaving Josephine in Marrakesh.

While there, Jack received a telegram:

JOSEPHINE OPERATED URGENTLY IN MARRAKESH. VERY SERIOUS. COME AT ONCE.

Immediately, he applied for authorization to visit, and twenty-four hours later he was once again at the foot of her hospital bed. Outside the hospital and all around the medina, prayers and chants could be heard for her recovery.

Jack was pacing the hospital corridor when he heard a commotion from the stairwell. He thought he heard Menehbi's raised voice and went to see what on earth was going on. As he descended the stairs, he saw Menehbi holding a goat which was bleating and several nurses trying to prevent him climbing up the stairs.

"Jack, I have to sacrifice the goat at the foot of Josephine's bed."

"No. She would never agree to that."

"But it is the only way to save her. I have visited a reputable soothsayer and he has told me I must follow his instructions exactly."

Jack didn't know what to do. He had witnessed many strange things in North Africa that he would never have believed possible. It was clear from his friend's fraught expression that he believed in his heart of hearts that the only way to save Josephine's life was to make the sacrifice. The crowd who had followed Menehbi into the hospital urged him on. Jack let out a deep breath. He too was prepared to do anything that might save Josephine. One of the nurses ran to collect an anesthetic for the goat. Menehbi agreed to make the sacrifice where he was, rather than in Josephine's hospital room. After the nurse had administered the injection, Menehbi said a prayer then slit the goat's throat with the knife he had brought for the purpose.

Chapter 68
ALGIERS 31 MAY 1944

Acting Sub-Lieutenant Baker, Josephine, is ordered to present herself, wherever her services are required. Motive – propaganda. Means of transport – all means. Qualified military authorities are requested to facilitate Sub-Lieutenant Baker's movements.

Signed: Air Force General Bouscat

6 JUNE 1944

Jack glanced at his watch. Seven in the morning, still plenty of time. The servant had assured him that Josephine and General Bouscat were in their final stages of preparation and would join him shortly. He lit a cigarette and wandered through the gardens of the General's house. Palm trees lined the elegant walkways. He turned attracted by a strange person at the gates of the residence. As the figure approached, he could see it was Zimmer, but his movements were outlandish as if he were a lunatic. He was almost dancing along the path towards him, waving his arms in an eccentric manner.

"It's happened," Zimmer shouted. "They landed this morning." He grabbed Jack's shoulders and shook him.

"Calm down. What are you talking about?"

Zimmer's eyes were wide with excitement as he explained, "I'm staying at the same hotel as some English soldiers. They woke me at five this morning with their noise. I went to see what the commotion was, and they were celebrating. The Allies have landed in Northern France."

Jack turned to Josephine and to General Bouscat who had just joined them. He picked Josephine up and twirled her in the air.

"Mon Dieu. I must tell my wife," General Bouscat muttered before rushing back into his residence.

"Is it really true?" Josephine asked, once Jack returned her to earth. "How come General Bouscat didn't know? He is the Air Commander of the Free French Forces?"

"Top secret." Zimmer laughed, swinging Josephine into a dance. "It's happening. The English soldiers were listening to the radio. I heard the reports. It's real."

Josephine choked back tears. "Home. We'll be able to go home soon." She glanced at Jack. Her dream was still waiting for her at Milandes. Perhaps she would not have to wait too much longer to get back there.

Jack glanced at his watch. "We need to get moving. We can celebrate properly in Corsica." Then in convoy, they left for the airport. On arrival, they walked onto the tarmac to inspect the plane. Zimmer walked around the Goéland aircraft assigned for their use. He had a worried expression. "I don't like this plane," he explained. "I prefer that one there." He nodded to the Glen Martin which was positioned alongside their proposed transport. Zimmer spoke to the General in a whisper, "It is with this plane that you expect us to get to Corsica?"

"Certainly, it is an excellent plane, and in addition I am providing our best pilot."

They boarded with some excitement. It would be the first time in four years they would set foot on French soil. Josephine and Zimmer each took one of the four armchairs in the passenger section. Jack sat in the cockpit with the pilot.

The plane flew over the Kabyle mountains. It was a clear morning with blue skies all around. The passengers sat in silence each preoccupied with thoughts of France and the events unfolding in Normandy. As they left the mountains behind for the azure blue of the Mediterranean, they heard a worrying sound from the left engine: spluttering and clanking. The pilot assured them they could continue with only one engine. The plane seemed to be travelling more and more slowly, and it was a considerable relief when the mountains of Corsica became visible on the skyline.

A Spitfire sped past close by. The pilot made a thumbs up and then swooped upwards. Others joined him for an acrobatic display, then they disappeared as suddenly as they had arrived.

The plane continued to lose altitude, and soon they found themselves flying between the mountains. It seemed impossible they could pass through safely, and they all fell silent as they watched the pilot put all his energy into controlling their height.

The plane surged and barely managed to scrape over the mountains. As they began to descend towards the sea, it was obvious they were going to have to crash land. Zimmer calmly wrapped the flag around Josephine.

"This will protect you," he said. Jack positioned himself in the doorway between the pilot and the passengers so he could shout a warning when the plane was about to hit the water. Josephine found herself mouthing the words of a popular song,

"Though there's one motor gone
We can still carry on
Comin' in on a wing and a prayer."

Although her ears hurt and her life seemed to be spinning around in her head, she felt strangely calm as the sea rushed towards them. She was sure it was not her time to die.

"Brace yourselves," Jack shouted.

Their bodies jolted as the plane hit the water. The engineer shattered a window with an axe, and they managed to crawl out of it on to the wing.

Josephine remained confident she would be safe because she had the flag of Lorraine wrapped around her French uniform.

The plane began to drift, and some of the soldiers on the shore swam out to greet them. One of them carried Josephine to land piggyback style. She was still draped in the Cross of Lorraine. Later they would try to rescue her stage costumes from the water, but many of them, especially the

wigs, were ruined. Josephine had made a spectacular entrance on her return to France, but not as planned.

Chapter 69
CHRISTMAS 1945

The thin covering of snow failed to disguise the debris of battle which lined the roads to Paris. Bombed out and abandoned tanks, twisted rail tracks, shells of cars were everywhere. The war might be over, but its repercussions would last forever. So many lives lost, and families destroyed. Starting to repair and rebuild what could be fixed and salvaged from the ruins that remained was a task for the determined. Jack sighed. He refused to become morose, especially as this Christmas promised to be a good one. Stationed temporarily in Marseille, he had managed to wangle a pass to allow him sufficient leave to visit Josephine in Paris. She was staying at a modest hotel until her house in Vesinet, which had been commandeered by the Germans during the occupation, had been put in a fit state for her return.

Running up the stairs and into the hotel reception, Jack was told that Josephine had left at four that morning. "You will find her at Les Halles or at La Villette. I believe that she goes to the markets to buy meat and vegetables. Yesterday she was out all day and did not return until nightfall." Jack let out a sigh. Either Josephine had become a requisitioner of food for a large organization or she had not changed. He travelled to Les Halles first, reckoning he was most likely to find her there. He picked her out immediately. She was such a distinctive figure in her navy-blue Air Force coat and white crocheted beret. She was gesticulating at some young butchers and already there was a row of packages wrapped in brown paper before her.

As he approached, she gave him a gleaming smile. "Jack, you've arrived just in time. Help me. Take these," placing a dozen or so parcels in his arms. "I'm parked

over there." She pointed to a grey Citroen near the entrance to the market. As Jack walked to the car, he thought he might have been annoyed if he was not used to her and knew what to expect. He had not travelled all the way from Marseille to be treated like a servant. She explained how she had negotiated for two hundred kilos of veal for the aged in the banlieue, a ton of vegetables and that she had also requisitioned, for the needy, a ton of coal which she had discovered in the basement of the building she owned in Avenue Bugeaud. Her tenants were incensed, but Josephine had told them. "It's my coal. It was bought by my factor, albeit with your rent. You are rich and can buy more coal. This coal will be of more benefit to the poor who have no means of heating."

That evening, they carried parcels to the neediest in each commune. The lists of people had been provided by the mayor of each district.

"Don't forget, this is a present from the Air Force of the Free French Forces," Josephine announced as she distributed each present. She showed them the Free French Forces buttons, which she had sown onto her coat in place of the Royal Air Force ones.

"They won't forget you," she would say. The coal was distributed by the mayors of each district again with the instruction that the beneficiaries were informed that the gift was from the Free French Forces.

Chapter 70

MILANDES, END OF
MARCH 1946

The car roared through the countryside as Jack pressed his foot on
the accelerator pushing the car to its limits. Josephine squealed in
delight. They would arrive soon. She couldn't wait to enter the valley
with the River Dordogne running between the cliffs on either side.
Had the river not given them lessons in courage? Had it not withstood
the English in the Hundred Years' War? Had not the knowledge of
this place and a need to return here helped them survive the hardships of the war years? It was a true French river, as beautiful as all of
France.

Finally, they saw the chateau towers through the trees. It was with
some trepidation that they drove through the gate. More than five
years had passed. The castle still stood guarding the valley, but bram-
bles had spread over the lawns and ivy had climbed over the walls,
covering the gargoyles. Wild roses had taken over the flower beds. As
if a scene from *Sleeping Beauty*. The castle may only have slept for five
years, but it could have been a hundred. They sat in silence taking in
the view, breathing the air, gazing over the valley. Here was the center
of her dreams, the home she had rented with the intention of making
it the place to raise her children. The war had snatched her dreams

from her, but now the war was over. It was time for her to realize her dreams. She had come back.

Briefly, they met the caretaker, and then Josephine led Jack to the library where a fire was already burning in the fireplace. They sat down on the spacious couches and watched the burning embers. As he watched the flames, Jack sensed a presence. Turning, he saw Zimmer had entered the room. Zimmer made a sign of silence and pointed to Josephine, who

had fallen asleep. "Quietly, quietly," he said. "She deserves some rest."

The two friends settled in their armchairs in front of the fire and exchanged adventures. The flames flared and Jack turned around to find that Josephine had disappeared. His heart filled with sadness. He had hoped the visit would signal the resurrection of their relationship which seemed to have come gently to an end as their respective military postings had taken them in different directions. The fire died down and he decided to retire. As he glanced at his armchair, he noticed a piece of paper. Picking it up he read, "Jack Sanders, you have been an inattentive companion. I hope you will remedy this tomorrow on the river."

And it is there that we will leave Jack and Josephine, in the shadow of Milandes, their skiffs gliding over the clear waters of the Dordogne, as they race towards Beynac and the apéro waiting for them at Madeleines.

Please go on to read the items in the Appendix. There are fictional accounts of Josephine's visit to a concentration camp shortly after its liberation and a description by one of her children of Milandes as it is today; some examples of the racial legislation imposed in the USA and by the Third Reich – there are many similarities; a timeline of Josephine's life, and some of the quotes attributed to her.

APPENDIX

1. Affidavit by Veronica Hope
2. A visit to Milandes 2019
3. Jim Crow Laws
4. Nuremberg Laws
5. Timeline Josephine Baker
6. Quotes attributed to Josephine Baker

AFFIDAVIT OF VERONICA HOPE

THE UNITED STATES WAR DEPARTMENT

WASHINGTON DC

I, Veronica Hope, former nurse in the Red Cross hereby certify that:

From 6 May 1943 to 18 August 1945, I was a nurse stationed with the Red Cross of Switzerland. my duties during that period were to accompany the Red Cross as directed in order to provide health and comfort where I could.

My unit was accompanying General Patton when he liberated the Concentration Camp of Buchenwald, Germany, on 11 April 1945.

I was in the front passenger seat of the lead Red Cross lorry when we entered the camp behind the American troops.

The entrance to the camp was through wrought iron gates with the words 'Jedem das Seine' forged into the design. I was later to learn that a translation of these words was 'everyone deserves what they get.' The camp was surrounded by a barbed wired fence approximately two meters high and with additional lines of barbed wire on the top. There was a guard tower above the entrance.

As we drove into the camp, we could see rows of wooden huts. There were prisoners wandering about – some were excited to see us and welcomed us enthusiastically although they were clearly weak. Others walked with eyes glazed as though drugged or in a daze. These prisoners seemed to have little awareness of what was happening around them. They were almost all very emaciated.

Then I became aware of the full horror of the situation. There were mounds of dead bodies littered around the central square. Other lone bodies lay sprawled on the ground where they had fallen. Some of the corpses had clearly been beaten severely, for others the cause of death was less obvious and could have been malnutrition or disease. The corpses were painfully thin.

We set to work unloading the trucks and trying to tend to the situation.

As a complete examination of the camp took place, the full horror of what had happened there began to become apparent, although it would be later before I became aware of all the atrocities which had been practiced there. Even after the liberation, despite our efforts, former prisoners were dying at a rate of around forty a day.

I and my colleagues located the infirmary, our primary focus being attention to the patients already in the hospital. I quickly realized that this was no ordinary hospital and that the facility was in fact a medical experimentation unit. There were no medicines left behind. All drugs and dressings, which might have been useful having been removed.

Lined on either side of each hut there were camp beds. These were occupied by prisoners who were unable to move. The medical conditions I treated included a man who had had his testicles removed. He described to me how the doctor who had carried out the castration had insisted on showing him a jar containing them after the operation. There were typhus victims and others who had been subjected to poison gas experiments and who had suffered side effects as a result. Almost all the prisoners very malnourished, their limbs painfully thin. Many had extended stomachs as a result of hunger. All were traumatized by the experiences they had been subjected to, and the brutality they had witnessed.

We immediately began to prepare to evacuate those patients who were strong enough to withstand the journey to a hospital. Many, however, were too ill to be moved, and others were clearly dying, our intervention coming too late to save them. These cases were particularly poignant. When the patients realized their ordeal was over and the camp had been liberated, a light would come to their eyes and with it a new energy. It broke my heart to watch this light fade, as did their life. as their bodies finally succumbed; all I could think was at least their suffering was at an end.

Although my duties were focused on the living, it was impossible to ignore the horror of the camp.

It had been an extermination camp and had housed only men, from all corners of Europe. Their nationality and a camp number had been tattooed on their stomachs. The survivors told me horrific tales of how occupants had been killed by being worked to death, being shot in the back of the neck, starvation, disease, torture and brutality. They wore striped camp uniforms. Some had overcoats. They were housed in huts. The huts stank, and were stacked with bunks where men slept up to five in each bunk.

Even those who were fit enough to be transferred suffered typically from starvation and infestation of lice and fleas, unavoidable in the cramped conditions.

While performing my duties at the camp, I also saw the ovens in the crematorium. Their disposal capacity apparently four hundred bodies per day. There was a row of ovens. The makers, J.A. Topf and Sons had placed their plaque on the wall. I saw charred human remains in the ovens and piles of human ash outside the building. I saw stacks of human bodies outside the crematorium where they had been abandoned. Words cannot describe the sight. Malnourished bodies were stacked nearly six feet high, legs and arms protruding randomly like matchsticks tossed to the ground. Eyes stared from the corpses accusingly. Never in all my years as a nurse have I witnessed such disregard for the human being.

Other discoveries at the camp were brought to my attention. Depravities included lampshades made of human skin, pictures painted on human skin, and human heads shrunk to one fifth of the normal size.

The day following the liberation, General Patton ordered that mostly male German citizens of military age, plus a few women, from the nearby town of Weimar tour the camp. They were forced to walk the five miles from the town to the camp. I remember watching the townspeople arrive. Generally speaking, they appeared well-dressed and well-fed. As they entered the gates, they were confident and jovial.

That soon changed as the atrocities were revealed to them. The General had insisted that the camp be left as it was found until the movie crews had filmed the evidence of what had happened. There would be the war commission afterwards, and therefore a need for preservation of evidence.

Many of the visiting women fainted and required treatment before they were able to leave for the five-mile return walk to their homes. Many claimed to have no knowledge of what was taking place at the camp, despite living in such proximity.

After the visit, and when the film crew had done its work, the burials began.

The US soldiers took charge of organization of the burials and the resettlement of the camp occupants.

I continued to be stationed in the infirmary and volunteered to stay with those patients who were too ill to be moved. It was then that we had some exciting news. We were told that Josephine Baker, the singer and dancer, intended to visit the camp.

Initially the Red Cross advised against the visit because of the risk of typhoid in the camp. we were told, however, that Miss Baker insisted on visiting.

I personally tried to prevent the visit, too, as I felt that the patients were too weak and would not benefit from having a celebrity such as Miss Baker in their midst.

I was wrong. Miss Baker arrived about two in the afternoon and immediately entered the infirmary. I spoke to her personally to warn her about the risk from typhoid and to explain how the disease could be spread.

She was wearing an Airforce topcoat when she arrived, but she took it off when she sang. She was wearing a glamorous blue dress with diamante detail at the waist. She looked very beautiful and made it possible to forget for a few moments where we were. Some of the patients cried when she sang. then she spent time chatting to many of them. She also sat with one who was dying and held his hand. Even though the patients were very ill, I could see that the visit by Miss Baker's visit had brought some comfort to them.

One or two noticeably brightened and sat up in their beds, determined to look the best for their famous visitor. I thanked Miss Baker at the end of her visit and reminded her to wash her hands immediately. I could see that she was not in the best of health herself. I was told by her entourage that she refused to stop and was determined to continue performing for allied troops and liberated prisoners until the war was completely over.

I stayed at the camp until the last patient was able to leave, and then returned to my home.

The last thing I did before leaving the camp was to visit the memorial to the tree of Goethe, which was inside the campgrounds, though only the stump remained. Goethe, who had been a resident of Weimar, had been in the habit of climbing the Ettersberg hill and walking to the tree. He had done some of his writings there. The tree had been destroyed by American bombing in 1944.

Some of the prisoners had described to me people having their arms tied behind their backs and then hung from the tree. This torture was called Strappado.

I could not understand how persons who could appreciate the great scholar could also inflict such cruelty upon their brothers in humanity.

The words of the Buchenwald oath sworn by a group of the camp survivors after they had risen up and overthrown their guards will be forever in my consciousness.

"We will cease our fight when the last guilty person stands before the judges of the people. The obliteration of Nazism as well as its roots is our guiding principal. The building of our new world of peace and freedom is our only goal. That is what we owe our murdered comrades and their families."

It is estimated that fifty-one thousand men and boys died in various ways at Buchenwald.

I swear that the words of the affidavit are true and indeed am bound to say that my words can never adequately describe the horrors I saw at Buchenwald. The pain and suffering I witnessed there will be forever scarred on my memory.

All of which is the truth. Sworn on this day, the 19th of May 1946.

MILANDES

1 July 2019

As I drove along the road towards Milandes, I could feel the years sliding away. Way back. As far back as I could remember. At first, the castle seemed strange with its carpark and signs for buses and cars, then the queue for tickets and the attendant handing me the audio equipment with brief but friendly instructions for its use.

I kept my eyes lowered and moved on. My place was taken immediately by the next person in the queue. I breathed in deeply as I gazed over the beautifully manicured lawns with their flowerbeds and fountain at the foot of the garden. Then my eyes turned to the castle. The ancient stone walls seemed less imposing then they had when I was a child. But I had grown and time had passed. It was only to be expected.

I walked towards the doorway. As I entered, I could hear the memories of my childhood as they tumbled through my consciousness. Laughter, tears, fights and reconciliations. They were all there. It was as I stepped through the doorway that I became overwhelmingly conscious of her presence, my mother. Her laughter followed me as I followed the directions for the tour, past cordoned-off areas where once I had run freely. No one paid any attention to me. I was one of the thousands of tourists who visited the chateau during the summer months. There was no reason for me to attract any particular attention. I was neither the spectacle nor the audience. I was a ghost who could drift unseen from room to room. I sat and watched the television programme which formed part of the tour. There I was as a child with my siblings leaving Milandes ... in Monaco ... at our mother's funeral. I choked back tears. I had never intended to return to this place. Yet here I was, and it still felt like home.

Happy memories wrapped around me as warm as the sunlight as I stepped out onto the lawns. I lay down on the grass and watched the falconry display. The birds swooped and dived with incredible beauty and skill as they must have done hundreds of years before for the count.

I allowed my body to sink into the grass. I could feel the anxieties which had prevented my return drift away into the soil. I felt at peace. She had taught us everything – everything except how to live without her.

JIM CROW LAWS ENACTED IN THE USA

1865. ARIZONA-Marriages between whites and blacks, 'mulattoes,' Indians or Mongolians were declared illegal.

1872. CALIFORNIA-The sale of alcohol to Indians was declared illegal.

1873. WEST VIRGINIA-Blacks prohibited from serving on juries. Overturned by legal challenge in 1880.

1875. RHODE ISLAND-Participants in an interracial marriage could be fined one thousand dollars or sentenced to six months imprisonment.

1889. NORTH CAROLINA-White and colored schools not to exchange books.

1904. MARYLAND-Railroad companies require to provide racially segregated cars or coaches.

1907. OKLAHOMA-Blacks prohibited from having the same hearses as whites.

1929. NEBRASKA-Marriage prohibited between a white person and a person of at least one-eighth Asian blood. The law was extended in 1943 to include anyone of at least one-eighth black, Japanese or Chinese blood.

1931. WYOMING-Schools directed to segregate their student bodies once 15 or more 'colored' children enrolled in a district.

1955. INDIANA-Race required to be identified on adoption petitions.

TENNESSEE-White and black patients required to be treated in separate buildings in hospitals for the insane.

1957. NEVADA- Gross misdemeanor for a white person to marry a person of black, brown or yellow race.

ANTI-JEWISH LEGISLATION

1933

MARCH 24 Statute passed enabling Hitler to make laws without the approval of parliament or the Reich president.

March 31 BERLIN -Jewish doctor's suspended from the city's charitable services.:

April 7 -All Jews removed from Government services. Jews forbidden from sitting the bar exam-required to become a lawyer. April 25. Numbers of Jewish students in public schools limited to a maximum of five percent.

July 14 Citizenship of Jewish people and 'undesirables' removed.

October 4 Jews banned from holding editorial positions.

1934

Jewish actors prohibited from performing on stage or screen.

Jews prevented from slaughtering animals-prevented adherence to Jewish dietary laws.

1935

May 21 Jews officers prohibited the army.

September 15 Nuremberg Laws introduced- excluded Jews from German citizenship or from marrying or having sex with German women. Jews were deprived of voting rights and the right to hold political office. Introduced the Mischling Test whereby individuals with at least one Jewish grandparent were considered Jewish.

1936

April 3 Jews prohibited from entering the veterinary profession.

October 15 Jewish teachers prohibited from teaching in public schools.

1937

April 9 Berlin excluded Jewish children from public schools.

1938

January 5 Jews prohibited from changing their names.

February 5 Jews prohibited from being auctioneers.

March 18 Jews prohibited from being gun merchants.

April 22 Jewish businesses prohibited from changing their names.

April 26. All Jewish people required to report all property worth over five thousand Reichsmarks.

July 11 Jews banned from health spas.

August 17 Jewish women required to adopt name Sara and Jewish men required to adopt name Israel.

October 5 All Jewish passports invalidated unless stamped with the letter 'J'.

November 12 All Jewish businesses required to close.

November 15 All Jewish children expelled from public schools.

November 29 Jews prohibited from keeping carrier pigeons.

December 14 All state contracts with Jewish owned firms cancelled.

December 21 Jews prohibited from being midwives.

1939

February 21 Jews required to surrender precious metals and stones in their possession.

August 1 Sale of lottery tickets to Jews outlawed.

JOSEPHINE BAKER TIMELINE

1906-3rd June- born Freda Josephine McDonald
  1912- begins working as a live in domestic.
  1919-marries Willie Wells-although Josephine's mother consents to the marriage it is not valid as a result of Josephine's age, begins touring with the Jones Family Band and the Dixie Steppers.
  1921-marries William Howard Baker.
  1922- performs in chorus line of Shuffle Along.
  1924-performs in chorus line of The Chocolate Dandies.
  1925-sails to France, performs in La Revue Negre.
  1926- performs at Folies Bergère, opens Chez Josephine.
  1927-stars in silent film Siren of the Tropics, Josephine's first biography Les
  Memoires de Josephine Baker is published, Josephine begins to work with Giuseppe (Pepito) Abatino, passes driving test, announces marriage to Pepito, campaigns for Bakerfix and Valaze Body Cream are launched with Josephine
  as model.
  1928-tour of Europe and South America.
  1929-Josephine and Pepito purchase Beau-Chene, in the Paris suburb of Vestinet.
  1930-Josephine is nominated as Queen of the Colonies for the 1931 Universal Colonial Exposition. The nomination is revoked because she is not a French citizen.
  1931-records J'ai Deux Amours, Mon Sang dans des Veines, a novella based on a story by Josephine is published.
  1932- stars in the revue La Joie de Paris, at the Casino de Paris, a record of the music from the show is released by Colombia featuring Josephine and her orchestra.
  1933- a further recording of the tunes from La Joie de Paris is released.
  1934-stars in film Zou Zou and later releases recordings of music from the
  film, takes lead role in performance of La Creole in Paris.

1935-stars in film Princess Tam Tam and releases records of music from the film, Josephine's collaborative biography Une Vie de Toutes les Coleurs is published

1936-performs in Ziegfield Follies on Broadway (only female black artist to do so),releases further recordings of music from Princess Tam Tam.

1937-returns to Paris, marries Jean Lion, becomes a French citizen, releases several records with Wal Berg and his orchestra.

1939-recruited by Deuxieme Bureau, performs in revue Paris-London

1940-stars in Fausse Alerte, moved to Château des Milandes after the invasion

of France, plays lead role in La Creole in Marseille.

1941-moves to North Africa, continues undercover work for Free French.

1942-divorce from Jean Lion becomes final.

1944-releases album with Jo Bouillon and his orchestra.

1946-awarded Medal of Resistance with Rosette by the French Government.

1947-marries Jo Bouillon, together they purchase Château des Milandes (previously rented).

1948-Josephine and Jo Bouillon tour United States. Thirty-six hotels refuse reservations for Josephine because she is black.

1949-performs Folies Bergere, Les Milandes opens as tourist attraction. Three recordings with Jo Bouillon and his orchestra are released.

1951-American tour, NAACP Woman of the Year, makes charges of racism against the Stork Club in Manhattan, FBI open files on Josephine.

1952-Josephine serves as goodwill ambassador for Juan Peron in Argentina for six months but leaves Argentian disillusioned. She is critized by U.S. officials and her South American tour is blocked. In Cuba her movements are restricted and she is placed under surveillance.

1953-records 'Dans mon Village.'

1954-tour North Africa.

1957-adopts Akio, Luis, Janot, Jean-Claude, Mosie, Brahim, Marianne and Jary, hosts Conferance Anti -Raciste at Les Milandes.

1958-adopts Mara, Koffi, and Stellina.

1959-adopts Noel, performs in Paris Mes Amours in Paris.

1960-Jo Bouillon leaves Milandes.

1961-Josephine decorated with the Legion d'Honneur and the Croix de Guerre with Palme at an official ceremony at Les Milandes.

1963- spoke at the March on Washington at the side of Rev. Martin Luther King. For her efforts as a civil rights activist, the NAACP name May 20th"Josephine Baker Day."

1964-Brigitte Bardot launches television campaign to save Les Milandes.

1966-performed in Cuba at invitation of Fidel Castro, album Josephine Baker en la Habana is released.

1968-invited by Coretta Scott King, after her husband's assassination to take over as leader of the Civil Rights Movement. Josephine refuses because of the age of her children, creditors seize Château des Milandes, performs at

Olympia in Paris, marches in support of De Gaulle.

1969- evicted from Milandes, performs at Chez Josephine, Paris.

1973- performs at Carnegie Hall and receives excellent reviews from critics. The show marks Baker's comeback as a performer. Tour of United States, Scandinavia and South Africa.

1974-performs at Royal Variety Performance at London Palladium

1975-performs at Bobino Theater in Paris. The performance is a celebration of the fiftieth anniversary of her debut in Paris. The audience includes Sophia Loren, Princess Grace of Monaco, Mick Jagger, Shirley Bassey, Diana Ross and

Lisa Minnelli.

On April 12, 1975, Josephine dies of a cerebral hemorrhage. At her funeral,

more than 20,000 people participate in the procession. The French Government provide her with a 21-gun salute, the first American born woman to be so honored. She is buried in Monacco.

ADDITIONAL INFORMATION

Jacques Abtey 1906-1998
Married Jacqueline in 1946 at Josephine's home in Paris
Wrote two books-
La Guerre secrète de Joséphine Baker, Éditions Siboney, 1948.
2e *Bureau contre Abwehr*, Paris, La Table Ronde, 1966.

Thami El Glaoui 1879 - 23 January 1956),
    Known in English as Lord of the Atlas, was the Pasha of Marrakesh from 1912 to 1956. He became one of the richest men in the world. He died during his night prayers on 23rd January 1956. His property and wealth was later seized by the state.
    Jo (Joseph) Bouillon (3 May 1908 – 9 July 1984)
    French composer, conductor and violinist. His band toured with Josephine. They married in the chapel at Milandes in 1947. The couple then proceeded to adopt twelve children of different 'races'. Josephine Baker and Bouillon separated in 1957 and divorced in 1961. Jo Bouillon retired to Argentina where he opened a French restaurant. He is buried with Josephine in Monaco.

Giuseppe Pepito Abatino 1886-1936

Former stone-mason from Sicily. Posed as a count. Met Josephine in Paris and persuaded her to allow him manage her. They became lovers. They could not marry as she was already married to Willie Baker. He organised many of her lucrative advertising contracts and lessons to aid her develop her career. The couple rowed during an American tour and he returned to France alone where he died.

QUOTES ATTRIBUTED TO JOSEPHINE BAKER

"The things we truly love stay with us always, locked in our hearts as long as life remains."

"I'm not intimidated by anyone. Everyone is made with two arms, two legs, a stomach and a head. Just think about that."

"He was my cream, and I was his coffee –And when you poured us together, it was something."

"Surely the day will come when color means nothing more than the skin tone, when religion is seen uniquely as
    a way to speak one's soul; when birth places have the weight of a throw of the dice and all men are born free,
    when understanding breeds love and brotherhood."

"...It looked very different from the Statue of Liberty, but what did that matter? What was the good of having
    the statue without the liberty, the freedom to go where one chose if one was held back by one's color? No, I
    preferred the Eiffel Tower, which made no promises."

"A violinist had a violin, a painter his palette. All I had was myself. I was the instrument that I must care for."

"Is that what they call a vocation, what you do with joy, as if you had fire in your heart, the devil in your body?"

"I wasn't really naked. I simply didn't have any clothes on."

"We must change the system of education and instruction. Unfortunately, history has shown us that brotherhood must be learned, when it should be natural."

"I like Frenchmen very much, because even when they insult you they do it so nicely."

'You are on the eve of a complete victory. You can't go wrong. The world is behind you.'

'I did take the blows, but I took them with my chin up, in dignity, because I so profoundly love and respect humanity.'

' I believe in prayer. It's the best way we have to draw strength from heaven.'

'We've got to show that blacks and whites are treated equally in the army. Otherwise, what's the point of waging war on Hitler ?'

' All of my life, I have maintained that the people of the world can learn to live together in peace if they are not brought up in prejudice.'

' Beautiful ? It's all a question of luck. I was born with good legs. As for the rest....beautiful, no. Amusing, yes.'

'The secret to the fountain of youth is to think youthful thoughts.'

' God dislikes evil, and no happiness can be built on hate. Love one another as brothers.

' Art is an elastic sort of love.'

' I have walked into the palaces of kings and queens and into the houses of presidents. And much more but I could not walk into a hotel in America and get a cup of coffee, and that made me mad.

'One day I realized I was living in a country where I was afraid to be black. It was only a country for white people. Not black. So I left. I had been suffocating in the United States...

A lot of us left, not because we wanted to leave, but because we couldn.t stand it anymore. I felt liberated in Paris.'

'The white imagination is sure something when it comes to blacks.'

-' Since I personified the savage on the stage, I tried to be as civilized as possible in daily life.'

'I was a devil in other countries, and I was a little devil in America, too.'
>

' I remember when Lindbergh arrived in Paris, I was one of the first persons to know about his landing, because as the French people knew that I was born in St. Louis, thinking I would be very proud to announce it to the public, they gave me the news first. I was then starring in the ' Folies Bergere.'

' The hate directed against the colored people here in St. Louis has always given me a sad feeling... How can you expect the world to believe in you and respect your preaching of

democracy when you yourself treat your colored brothers as you do ?'

' I wanted to get far away from those who believed in cruelty, so then I went to France, a land of true freedom, democracy, equality and fraternity.'

'Friends, to me for years St. Louis represented a city of fear....humiliation....misery and terror..

A city where in the eyes of the white man a Negro should know his place and better stay in it.'

' I shall dance all my life........I would like to die, breathless, spent at the end of a dance.'

ALSO BY EILIDH MCGINNESS

I hope you have enjoyed reading this book. Please take the time to leave a review. It only takes a minute or two of your time to leave a short review. It is a great way of providing feedback and encouragement for new authors. It can also really help with sales.

If you enjoyed JOSEPHINE, singer, dancer, soldier, spy- Please check out
THE CYPHER BUREAU
By
Eilidh McGinnes
Inspired by the life of Marian Rejewski-the Polish mathematician who first solved the Enigma code and passed the secret to the British and French.

PRAISE FOR THE CYPHER BUREAU

CAPTIVATING, COMPELLING, FACINATING
Although I was aware the Enigma had been broken by Poles, I didn't know any of the characters responsible or their stories. You brought them all to life in a captivating book, where facts, emotions, and the

hardships of their struggle were compelling. The epilogue was also fascinating.

Iain Bayne, Runrig

Although readers around the world are familiar with the accomplishments of Alan Turing and the British code-breaking team at Bletchley Park – most recently popularized in the Benedict Cumberbatch movie, The Imitation Game – the substantial contribution of Polish mathematicians to the unraveling of the Nazis' Enigma code is less well known. In The Cypher Bureau, Eilidh McGinness has written an exciting and forthright novelisation of the life of Polish mathematician Marian Rejewski and his colleagues, in an attempt to fill this historical blank spot.

As children, Rejewski and his two friends and fellow mathematicians, Henry Zygalski and Jerzy Rozycki, lived through the German occupation and depredations of World War I. Now, on the cusp of completing their university studies, war clouds are once again amassing on their country's western border. Polish authorities, fully cognizant of the Nazis' existential threat to their nation, are in search of expert minds who can expose the Germans' secrets and help foil their plans. They find these three young men.

Rejewski, Zygalski, and Rozycki are successfully recruited to work for the Cypher Bureau, although the danger of such work as the Nazi invasion looms. They have successfully solved numerous important decryption problems, yet Rejewski longs for a chance to try cracking Enigma – the coding machine the Germans considered unbreakable. Finally, he gets this super-secret assignment. Thanks to documents obtained by French intelligence and the lucky acquisition of an Enigma machine, he is able to reconstruct its internal wiring. Once that is accomplished, the method for decoding messages on a given day becomes relatively simple.

The insight that allows his breakthrough is not mathematical or technical, it is psychological. Having had German tutors in his youth, Rejewski knows how they think, and he applies their mode of thought to understanding the master codes that change daily. As the author of the book on which The Imitation Game was based wrote, "They had not broken the machine, they had beaten the system." Once Germany invades Poland, the code-breaking team must flee, working its way across Europe, stopping briefly here and there to decode messages, deal with Germany's increasing efforts to make Enigma more complex and, therefore, more secure, and making hair's-breadth escapes from their pursuers. It is dangerous work, and they cannot be certain whom to trust. In that way, although this aims to be a true account and is never hyperbolic, it reads much like an action thriller.

What is abundantly clear is the author's sincere respect for the bravery and the intellectual contributions of the Poles and a sense of the three mathematicians and the people around them as individuals. What's also clear is the commitment of a great many people in Poland and France, especially, to keeping the secret of the cypher team's accomplishments. Not one person ever revealed this information, and throughout the long years of the War, the Germans never knew they'd been hacked. This in itself is an astonishing feat. Until rather recently, the Poles' contribution to the penetration of Enigma's secrets was rather overshadowed. Today, however, it is better-known, and this book, though a novel, should aid in helping Rejerski, Zygalski, Rozycki, and the Polish cypher team take their proper place in history.

Vicki Weisfield Crime Fiction Lover

Anyone who has read Robert Harris's Enigma or anything else connected to Bletchley Park in WW2 would recognise the code breaking described here. This is, however, a book about the Polish team who originally decoded Enigma in 1932.

The man whose life we follow from his childhood to his death is Marian Rejewski. He joins a team of talented mathematicians at Poznan University who are inducted into Cryptography and asked to become secret code breakers. The story is very convincingly it shows the travails of this team. The author makes it clear that this is a work of fiction, but the details of events seem very accurate. The men have to leave their families when the Germans invade and move from place to place in Europe and North Africa, always working on code breaking. The intensity of their efforts in the face of enemy attacks and with the constant fear of betrayal is palpable. It seems that the Germans never realised that their code had been broken but their constant updating of the system caused a huge amount of work for the decoders.

I liked the way that the enormous Polish and French contribution to the decoding of Enigma messages was made clear. Indeed, without their work there would have been a far greater loss of life in WW2. You could describe this as a thriller with considerable technical input about decoding or as a biography of a Polish mathematician through WW2. A coda to the book brings the story of the decoders up to date. For anyone interested in this topic and in the hardships of WW2 this book is fascinating.

PROMOTING CRIME FICTION BLOG SPOT - JENNIFER S PALMER

ACKNOWLEDGEMENTS

Thank you to Alan Hamilton for his editing services and 'licarto' at 99 Designs for design of the book cover and to Ann Fraser and Alison Simpson for their beta-reading.

In the course of my research for this novel I have referred to the following books which proved invaluable.

Josephine By Josephine Baker and Jo Bouillon published by Paragon House Publishers

La Guerre secrète de Josephine Baker, by Jacques Abtey, published by Siboney, 1948.

Josephine Baker contra Hitler by Charles Onana published by Duboiris 2006

Josephine Baker in art and life, by Bennetta Jules-Rosette, published by University of Illinois Press 2007

ABOUT THE AUTHOR

Eilidh Mcginness is an emerging author of historical fiction. This is Eilidh's second book in this genre.

Eilidh was born and brought up in the Highlands of Scotland. She studied law at Aberdeen University, Scotland. She practiced law for fourteen years, latterly specializing in Criminal Defense. She then moved to South West France where she now lives.

Eilidh has always had a passion for history and is fascinated by seemingly ordinary people who achieve extra-ordinary things.

Eilidh loves to hear from readers so please say hello or join her on social media where you can keep up to date with offers, giveaways and new releases.

Printed in Poland
by Amazon Fulfillment
Poland Sp. z o.o., Wrocław

56564882R00175